WILSON DIARY

Peter Bialobrzeski

March 9 – March 26, 2023

Hartmann books

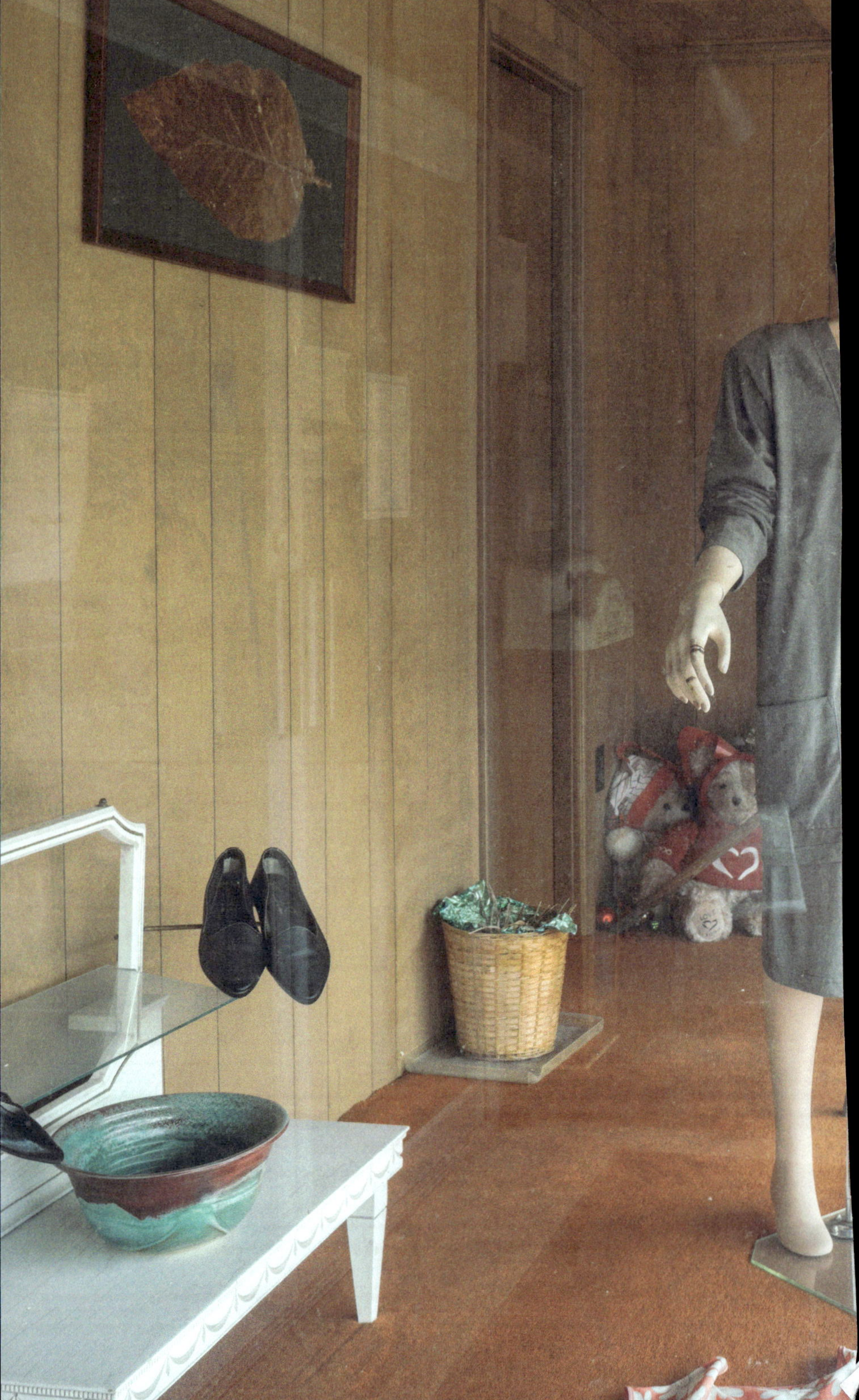

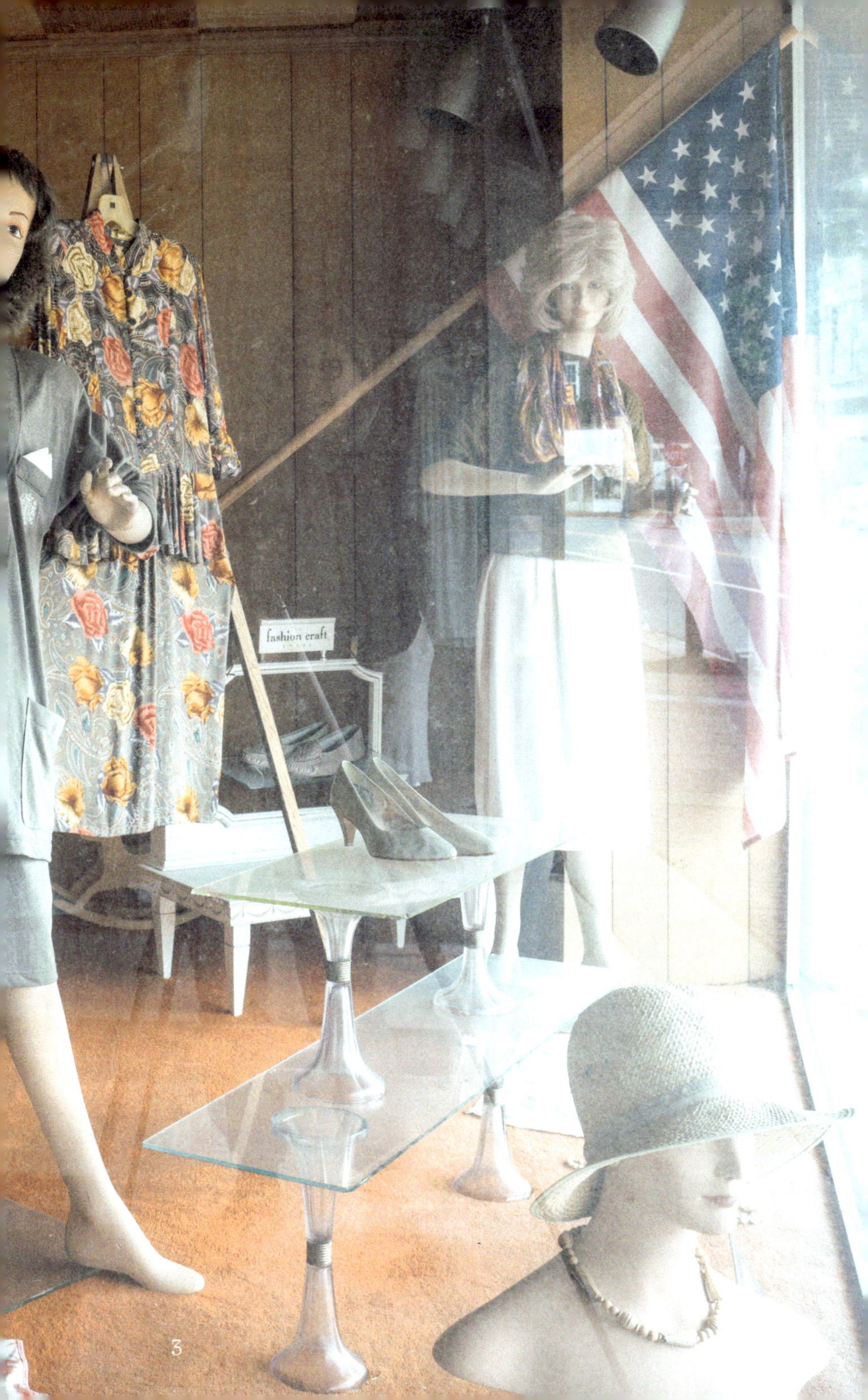
fashion craft

WILSON DIARY
Peter Bialobrzeski

→ March 9, 2023 I am staying in a warehouse, next to a local brewery run by a friendly giant who produces fifteen different types of beer, which are all served on tap. He does not miss the chance to give his babies names that are quite often as long as entire sentences: *Fiesta, Fiesta Del Fuego* or *Eastern Carolina Honey Blonde.* My favorite: *Busy Gettin' Phizzy Citrus Hard Seltzer.* Also tastewise. Oh, and the warehouse has been converted into apartments. It looks cool, but something went wrong: When the neighbors are talking on the phone, you can hear every word. And not just that. → March 10, 2023 It is a quiet town, a very quiet town. Well, except for those monstrous XXL SUVs with their up to eight cylinders and 400+ horsepower. Normally those things are supposed to purr like a kitten, but some DIY fanatic must have fiddled with the exhaust of most of the beasts that rise as early as I do. Most of them consume up to twenty-five liters of gas for every hundred kilometers. → March 11, 2023 No one seems to be moving on foot, except for two ladies walking the deserted streets of downtown in their jogging suits. They give me a thumbs-up while only two minutes later a builder dressed in a jumpsuit covered with spots of old paint, stops his bicycle and asks me what I am doing. When I explain, he declares that this is a good job, smiles, and gives me my second thumbs-up up within a few minutes. I can't do anything, but agree.
→ March 12, 2023 On the outskirts of downtown, many empty single-family homes look like something out of a Stephen King novel. Beautiful structures left behind by their owners, some for sale, others boarded up before they're eventually torn down. Some streets have more empty lots between abandoned houses than occupied buildings. The gray morning adds to the eerie atmosphere when suddenly a man behind me starts shouting: "Stay safe!" → March 13, 2023 Wilson, according to the website *historicdowntownwilson.com*, "is a thriving city of almost 50,000 people that has successfully recruited new business to replace the lost tobacco market revenue. During the heyday of the tobacco market in the late 1800s and early 1900s, its success drew prosperous farmers and businessmen to establish majestic homes downtown. Historically preserved architecture with high-speed fiber-optic internet blends the visions of yesteryear with the inspiration of tomorrow." This marketing speech does not match my observations and feelings.
→ March 15, 2023 Although there is a severe lack of things people like to have around, such as restaurants, cafés, and supermarkets, there is no shortage of houses of God. Eighty churches of different denominations are represented in

the city. →March 16, 2023 Last night the *Casita Brewing Company* hosted a music event. Various bands played rock and funk music that most of the musicians obviously grew up with. It had a 1970s feel to it, for a moment I thought it was just old people there, then I slowly realized it was my age group enjoying themselves. Apart from for one guy playing bass, there were only two or three black people in the room. At forty-eight percent of the population, the black community is the largest ethnic group in this former tobacco town, outnumbering whites by seven percent.
→March 17, 2023 Today, as every Friday, the biweekly print edition of the *Wilson Times* is on sale. The paper, founded as a weekly in 1867 under the name *Zion's Landmark* by Elder P. D. Gold, the pastor of Wilson Primitive Baptist Church, is my valuable source of background information. I learn that police have arrested a man suspected of committing a first-degree shooting in the parking lot of the *Walmart* where I regularly shop.
→March 19, 2023 Over the past few days, the temperature has ranged from under zero degrees Celsius to as high as twenty-three. In the early evening, an exhausted-looking man sits on a bench in an empty lot between storefronts and the last remaining houses. "I'm always tired," he says, and asks if I would take his picture. He thanks me when I do and says, "Stay warm" before continuing on his way into the unknown.
→March 20, 2023 Today, the local paper reports about a derelict building that Wilson Downtown Properties is purchasing. I had photographed the wooden structure on my first day in Wilson without registering its significance. According to a local source B. B. King stayed at the *Orange Hotel* in it's better days when he played in Wilson. It is a witness to a different era when "...you had cars on the road it was booming, booming. They had four or five cab stands, five or six restaurants and pool rooms." In short, a very far cry from today. →March 24, 2023 Sadly, I learn from today's *Wilson Times* that I will miss the *Johnny Cash Tribute Show* scheduled for April. *The Edna Boykin Cultural Center,* a building I had so far overlooked, already hosted the *Michael Jackson Tribute Show* in January. The theater was home to stars including Ava Gardner and Cary Grant, 3D movies and Saturday morning cartoons, serials and newsreels. →March 26, 2023 On the way home, I see an old Jaguar parked next to the entrance to my temporary home. The hood ornament depicts this very animal, and I can't help but feel a sense of connection. The rear window reads *Bright eyes chubby thighs*, and I wonder if that's really meant to refer to the headlights and body of this beautiful car.

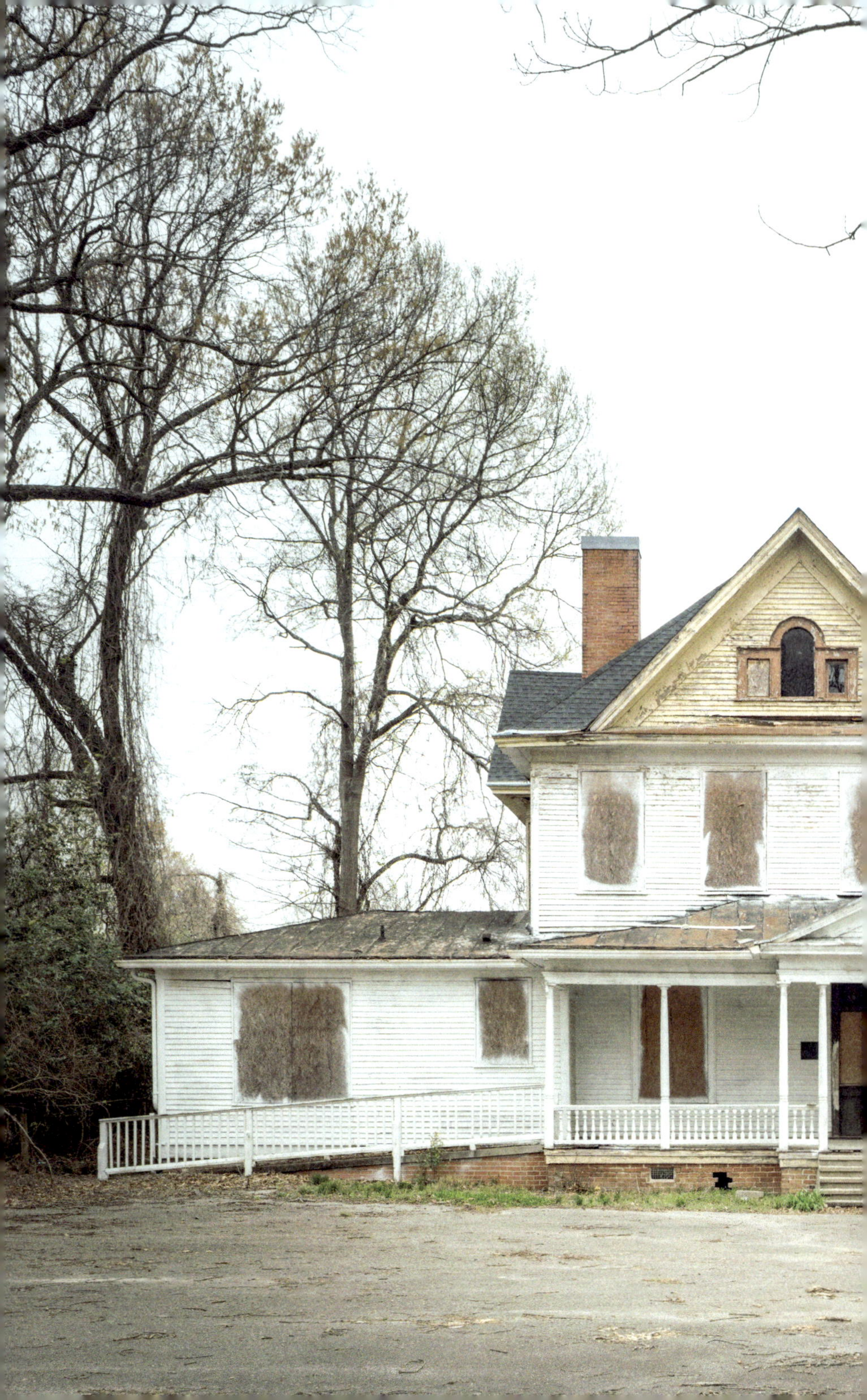

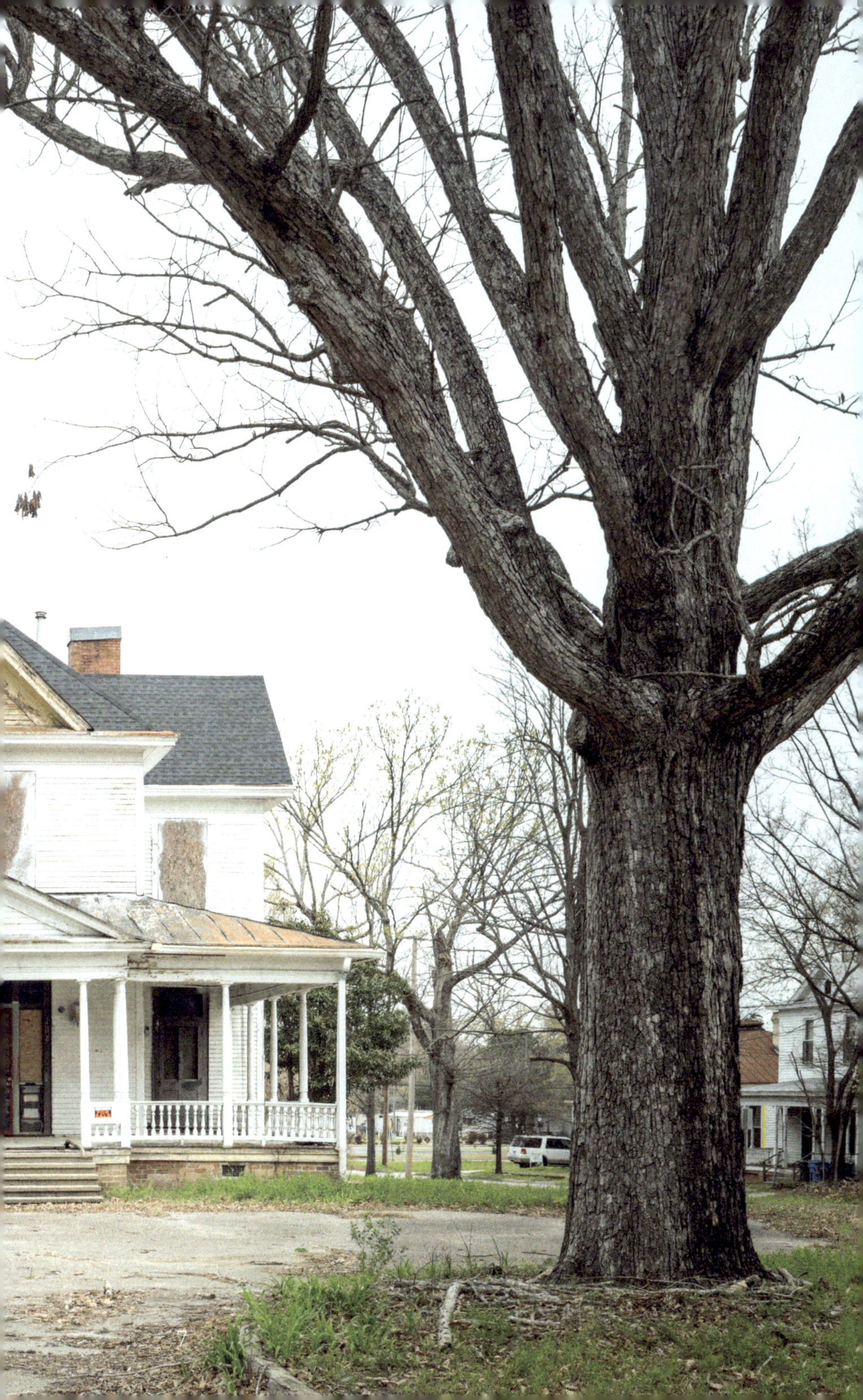

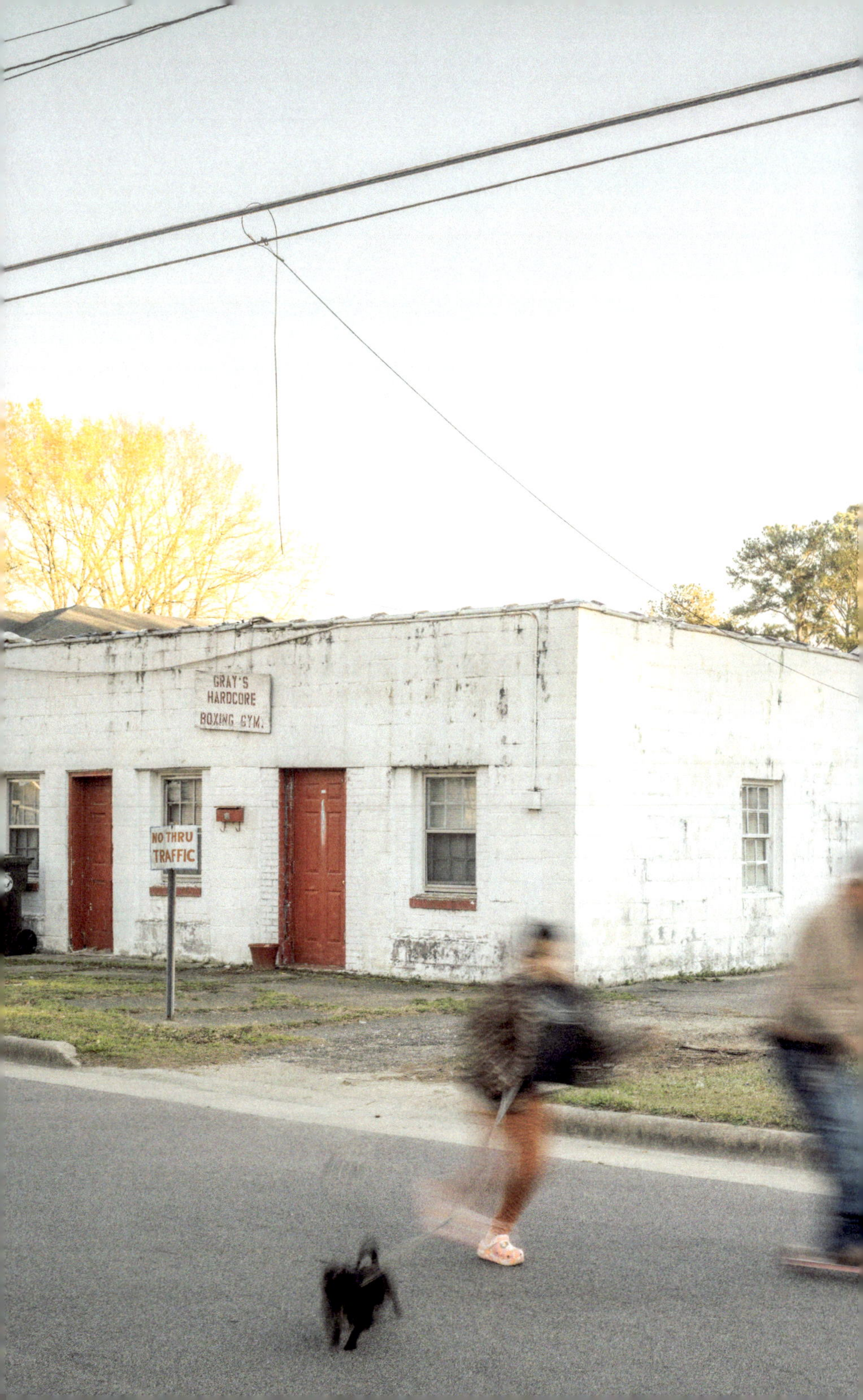
GRAY'S
HARDCORE
BOXING GYM.
NO THRU
TRAFFIC

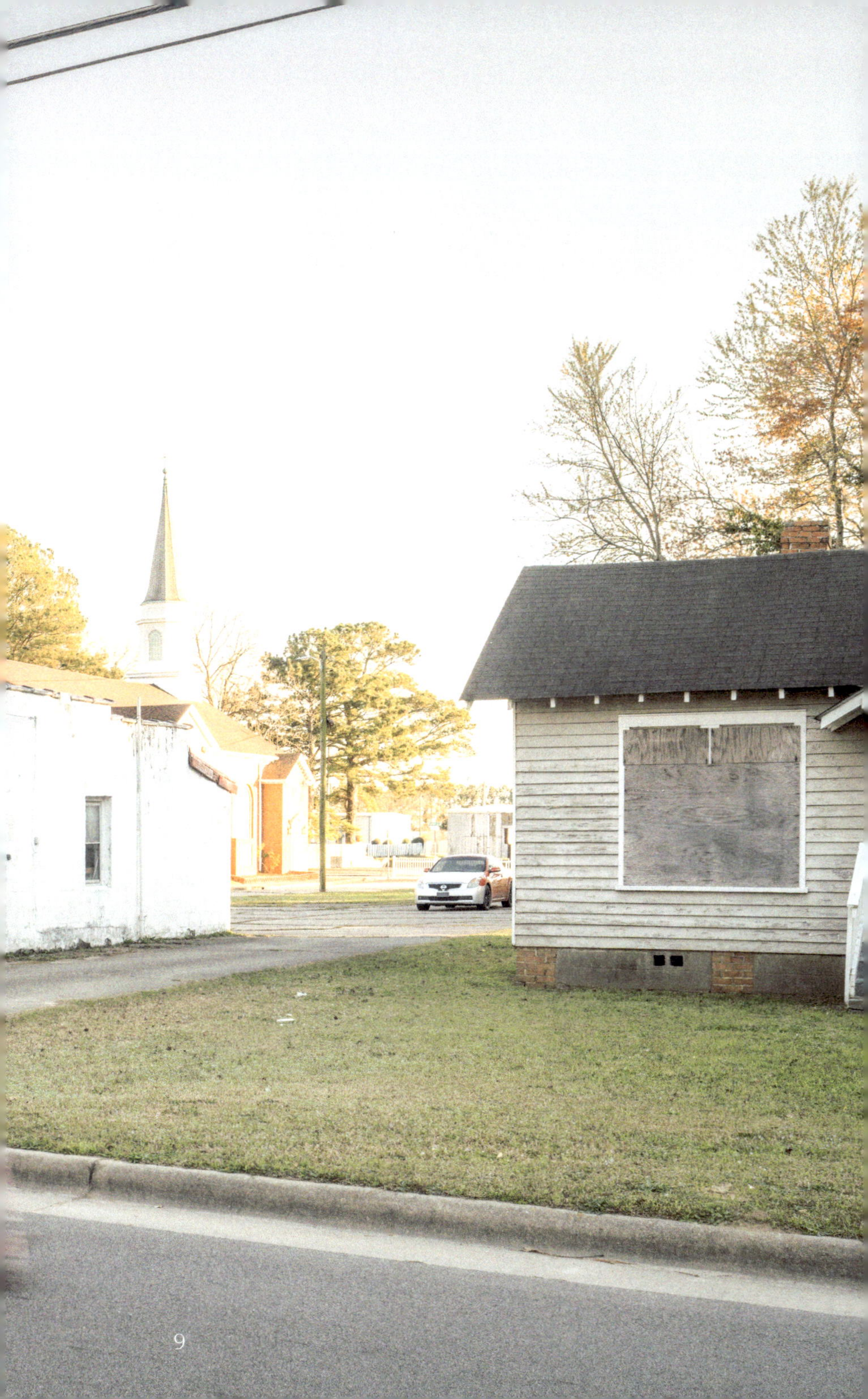

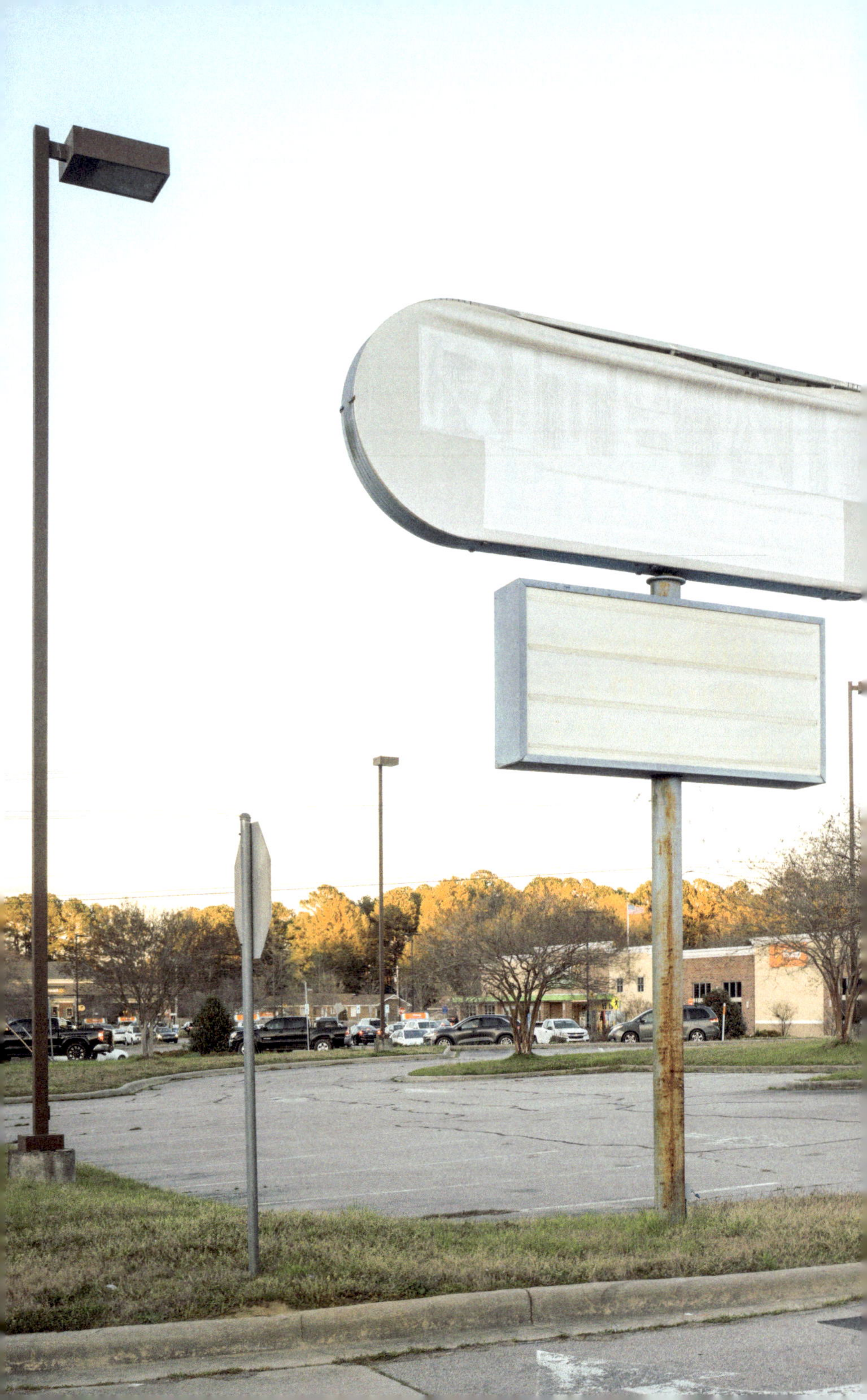

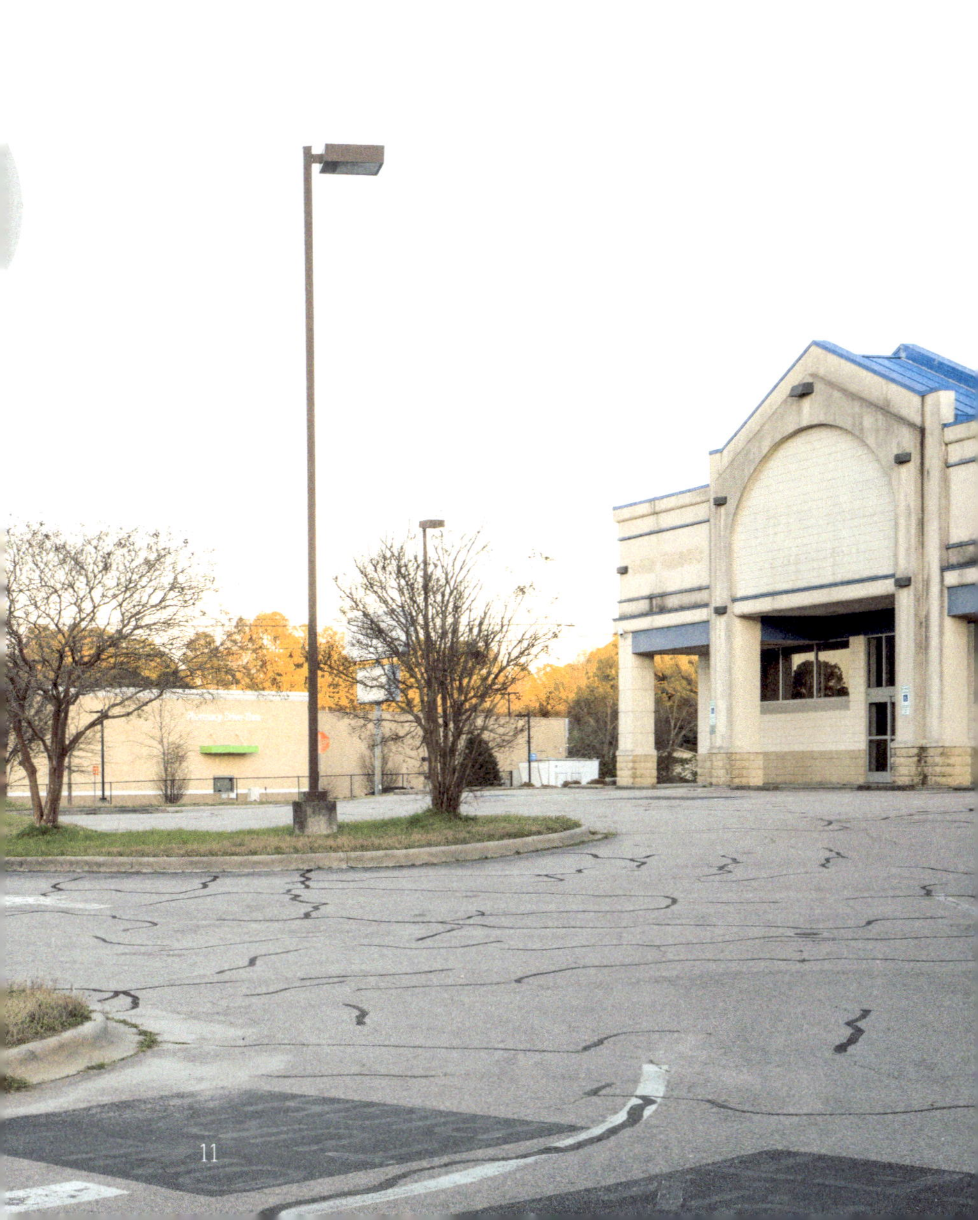

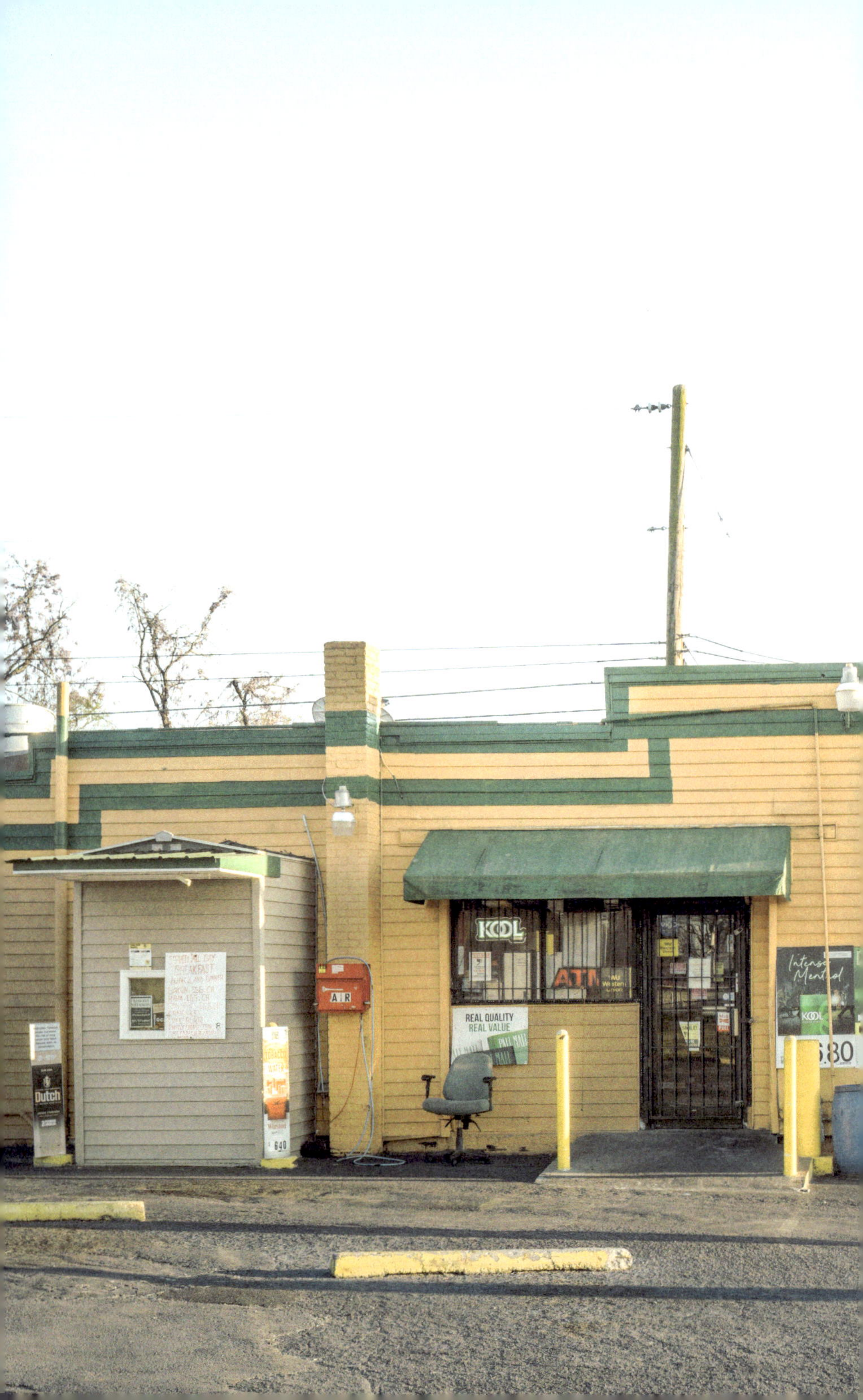
KOOL
ATM
AIR
REAL QUALITY
REAL VALUE
Dutch

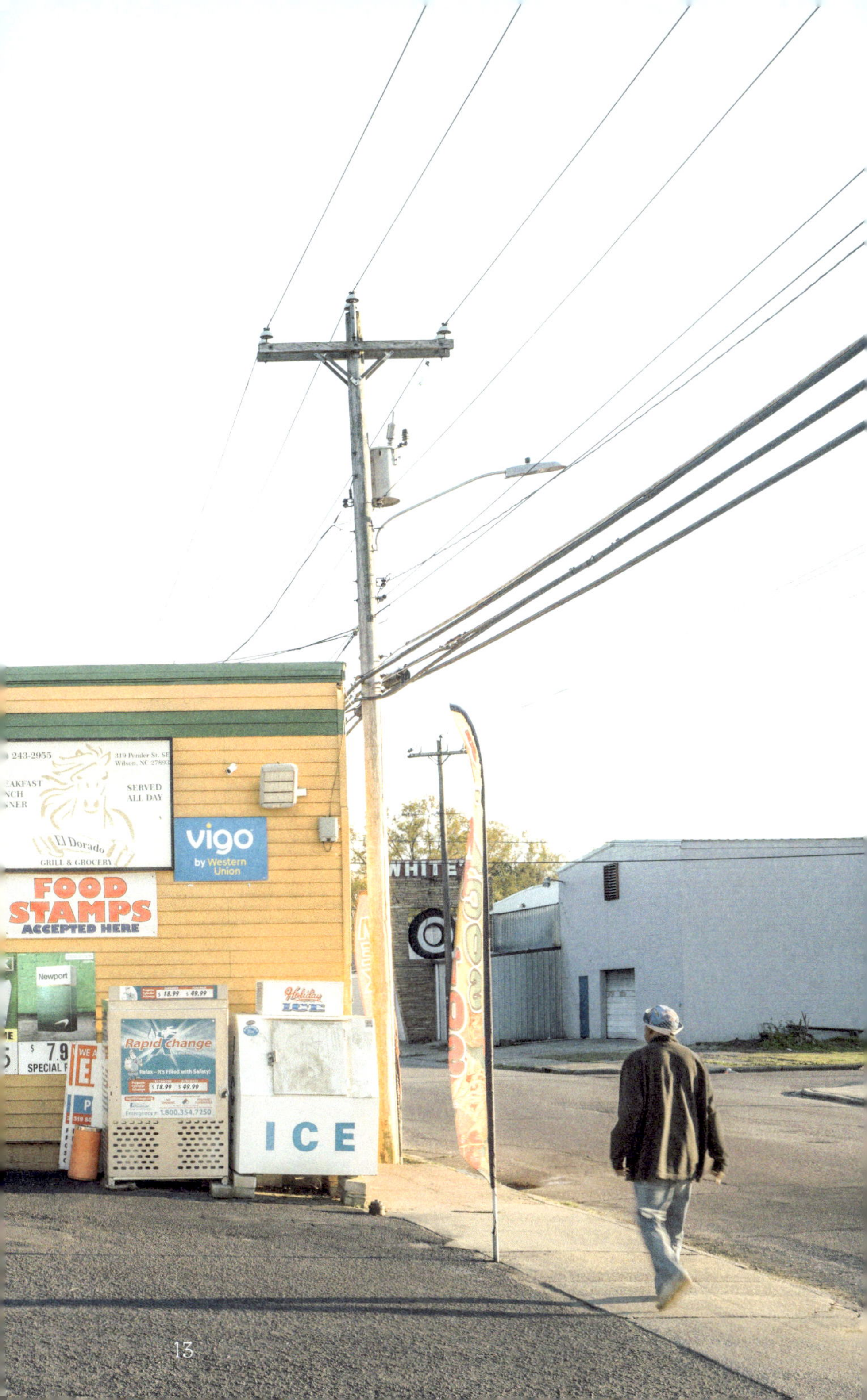
243-2955
319 Pender St. SE
Wilson, NC 27893
SERVED
ALL DAY
El Dorado
GRILL & GROCERY
vigo
by Western Union
FOOD
STAMPS
ACCEPTED HERE
Newport
Rapid change
Relax—It's Filled with Safety!
1.800.354.7250
Holiday
ICE
ICE
WHITE

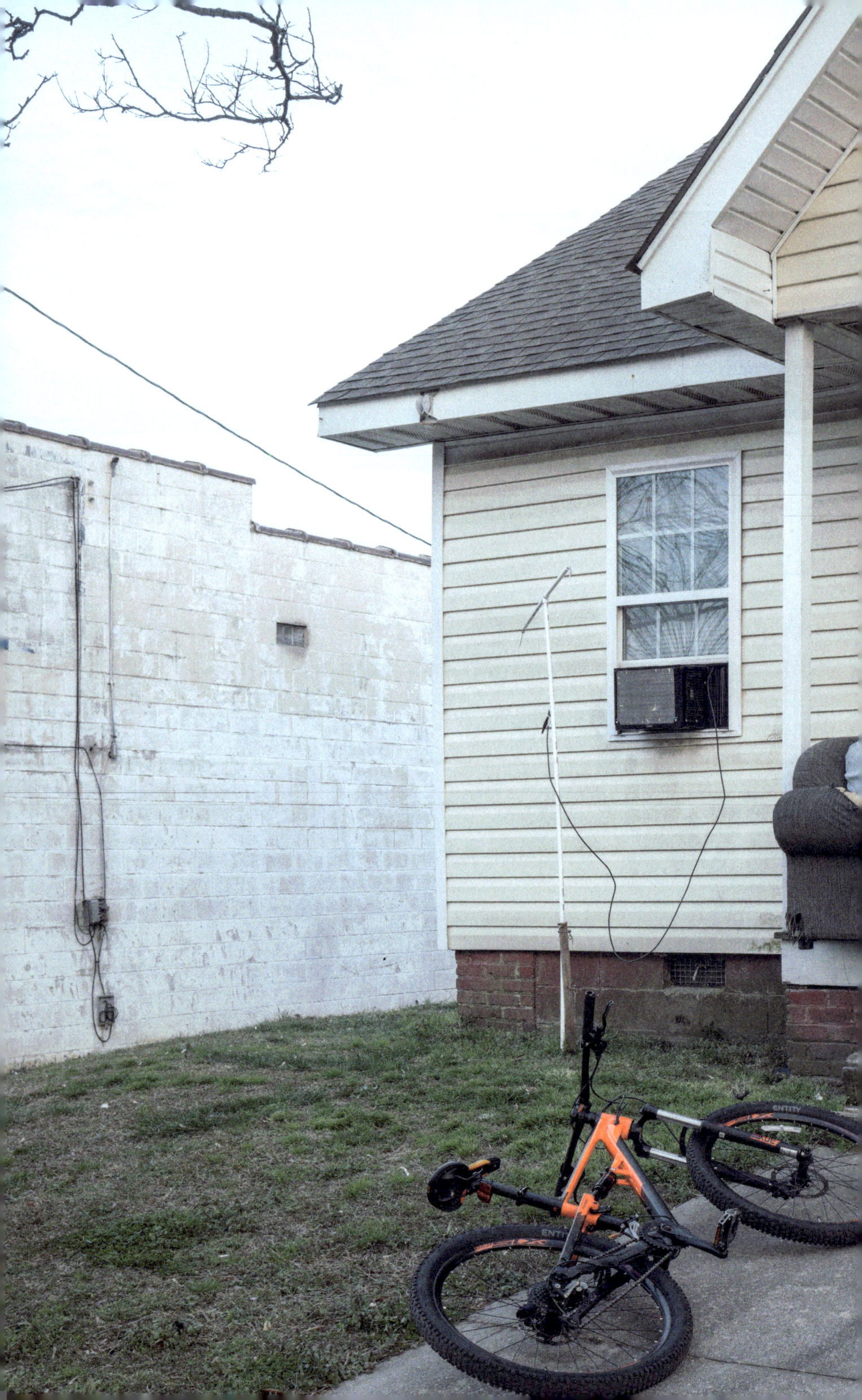
ENTITY

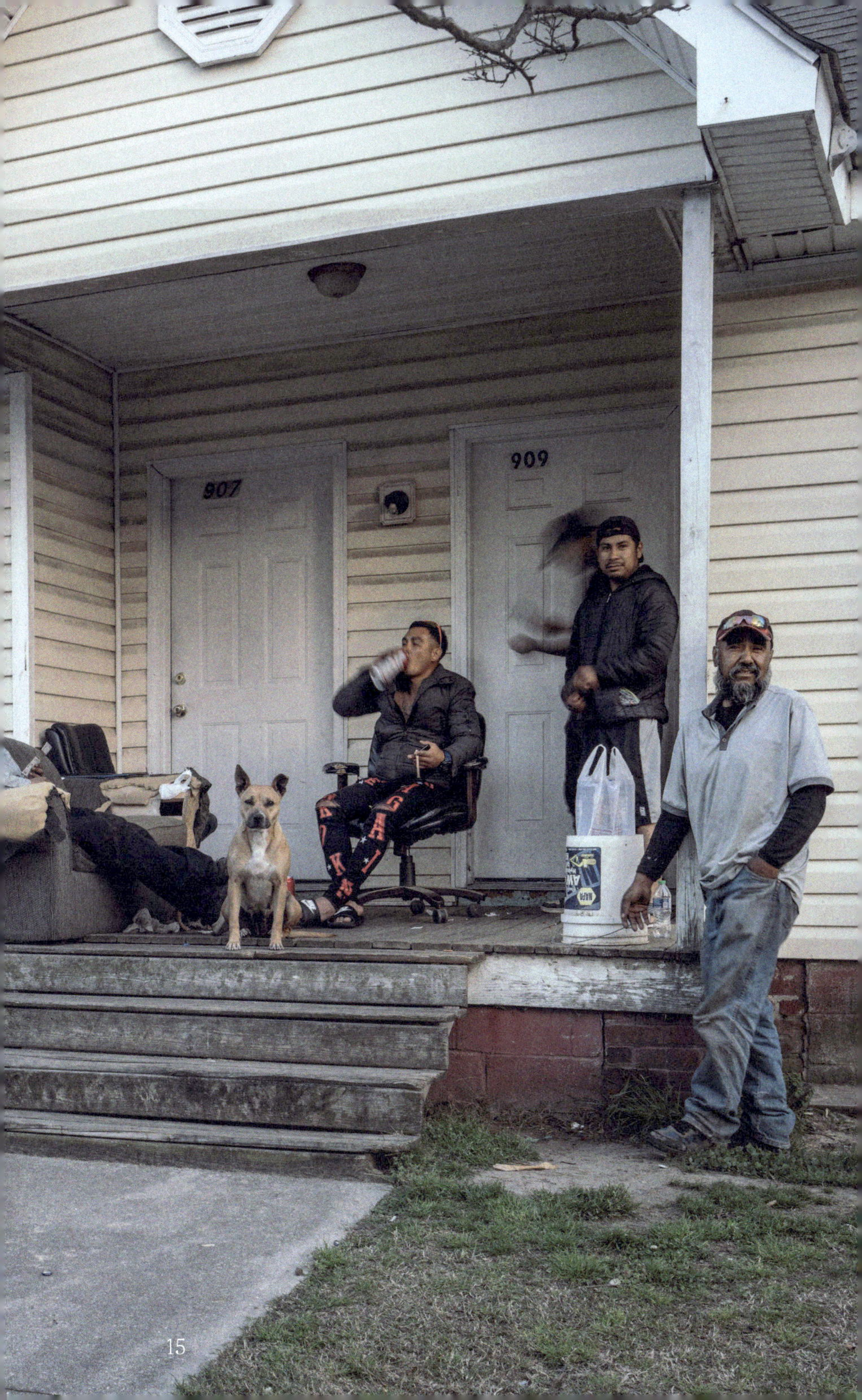
907
909

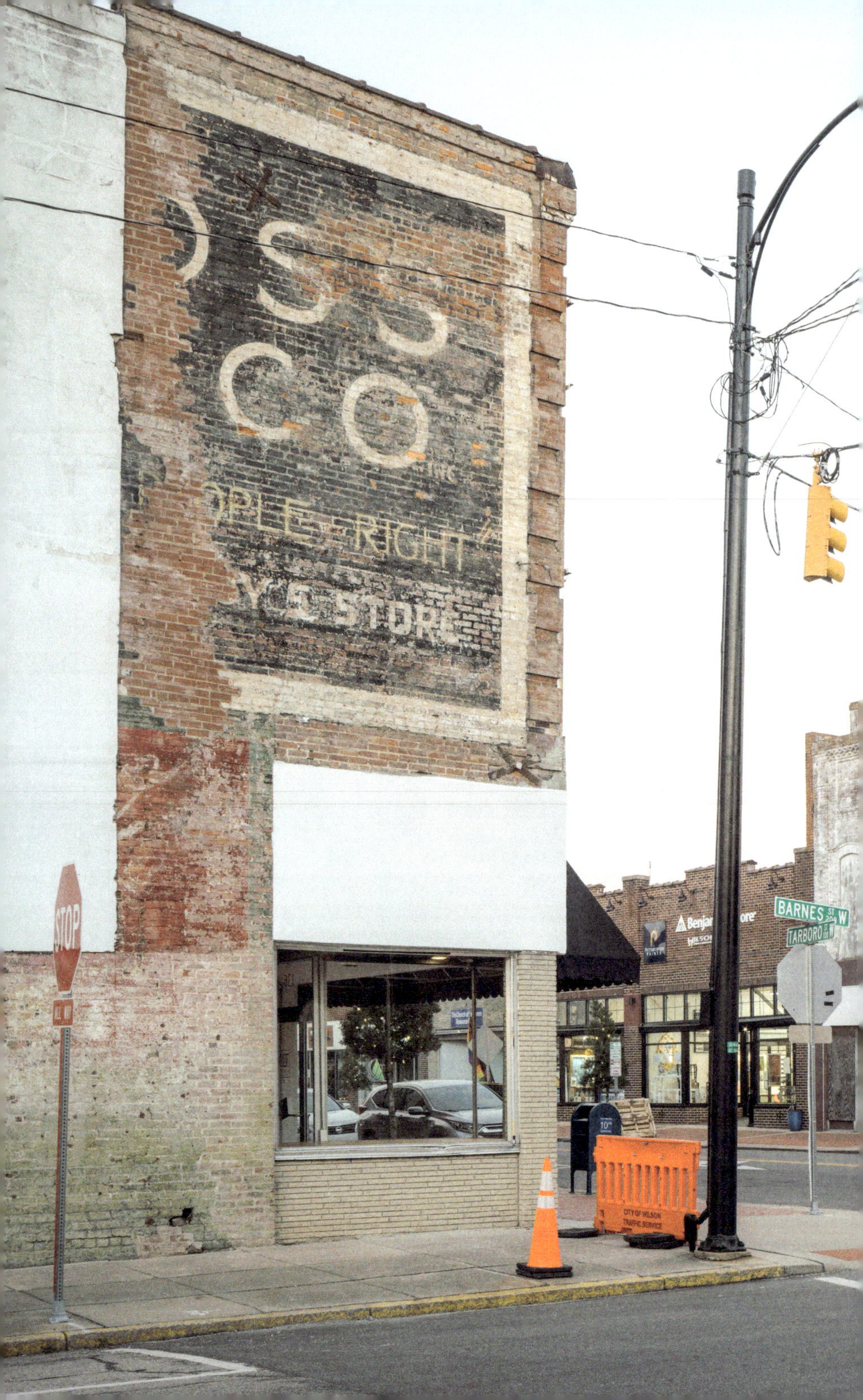
CO
STORE
STOP
BARNES ST W
TARBORO ST W
CITY OF WILSON
TRAFFIC SERVICE

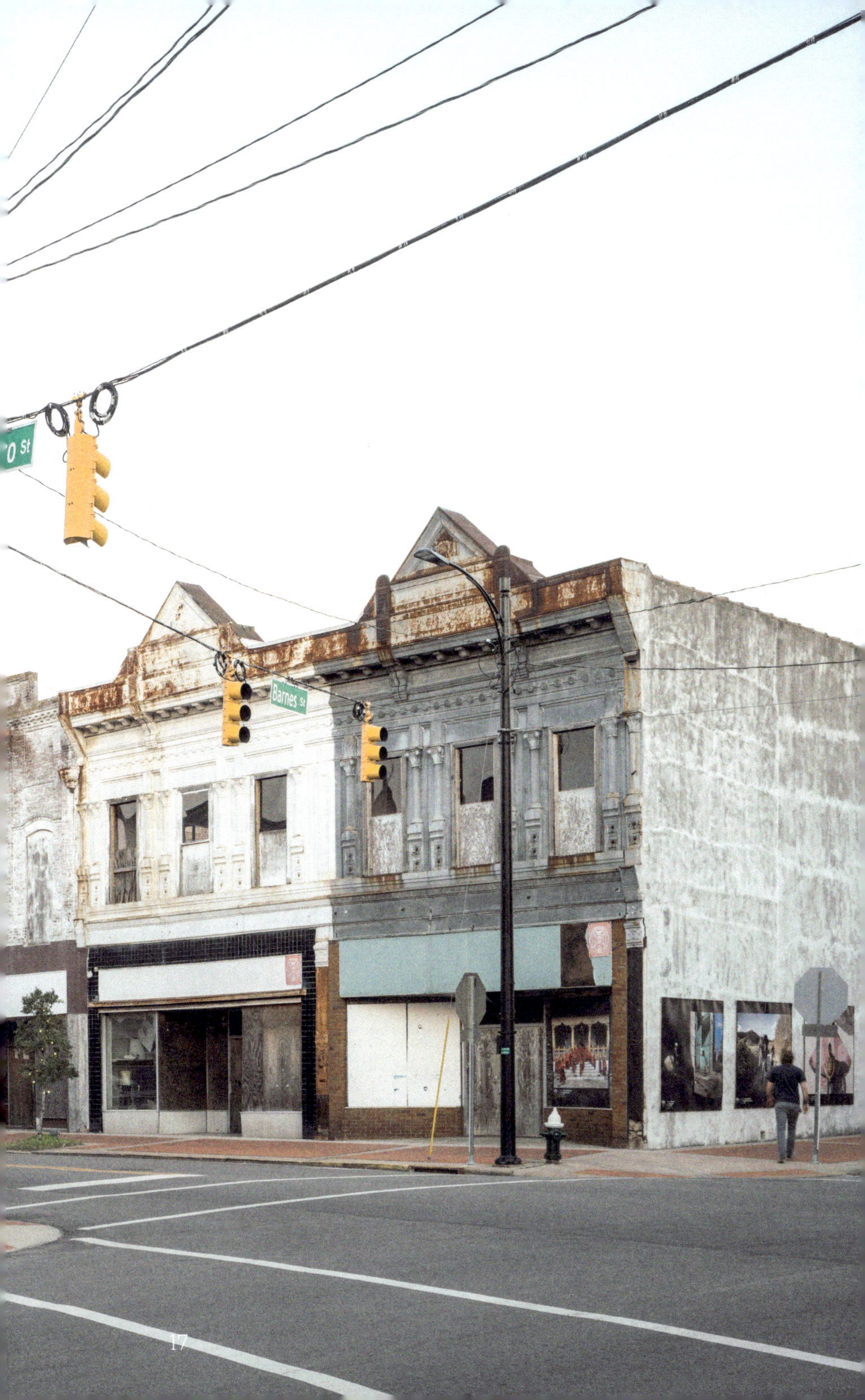
Barnes St

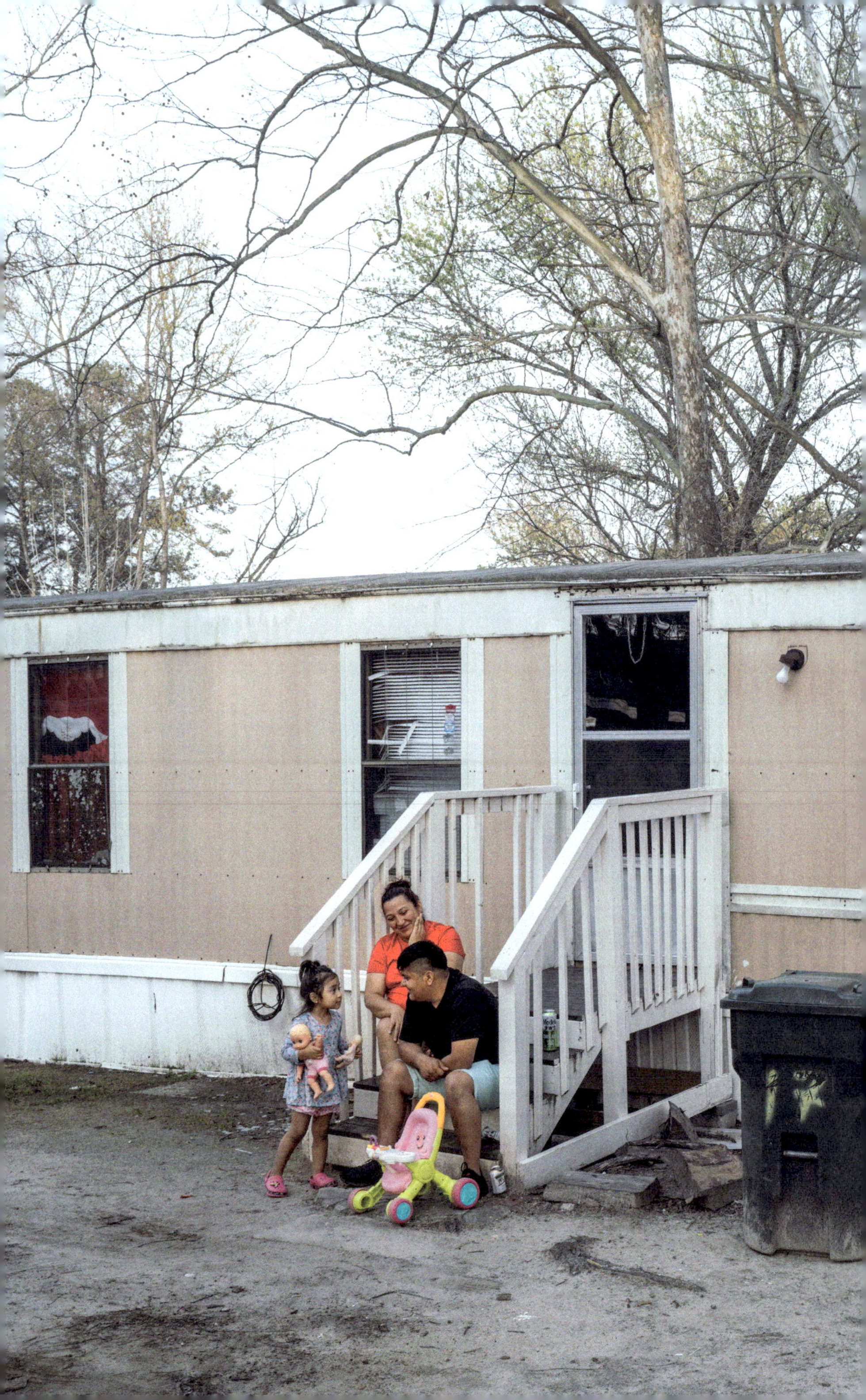

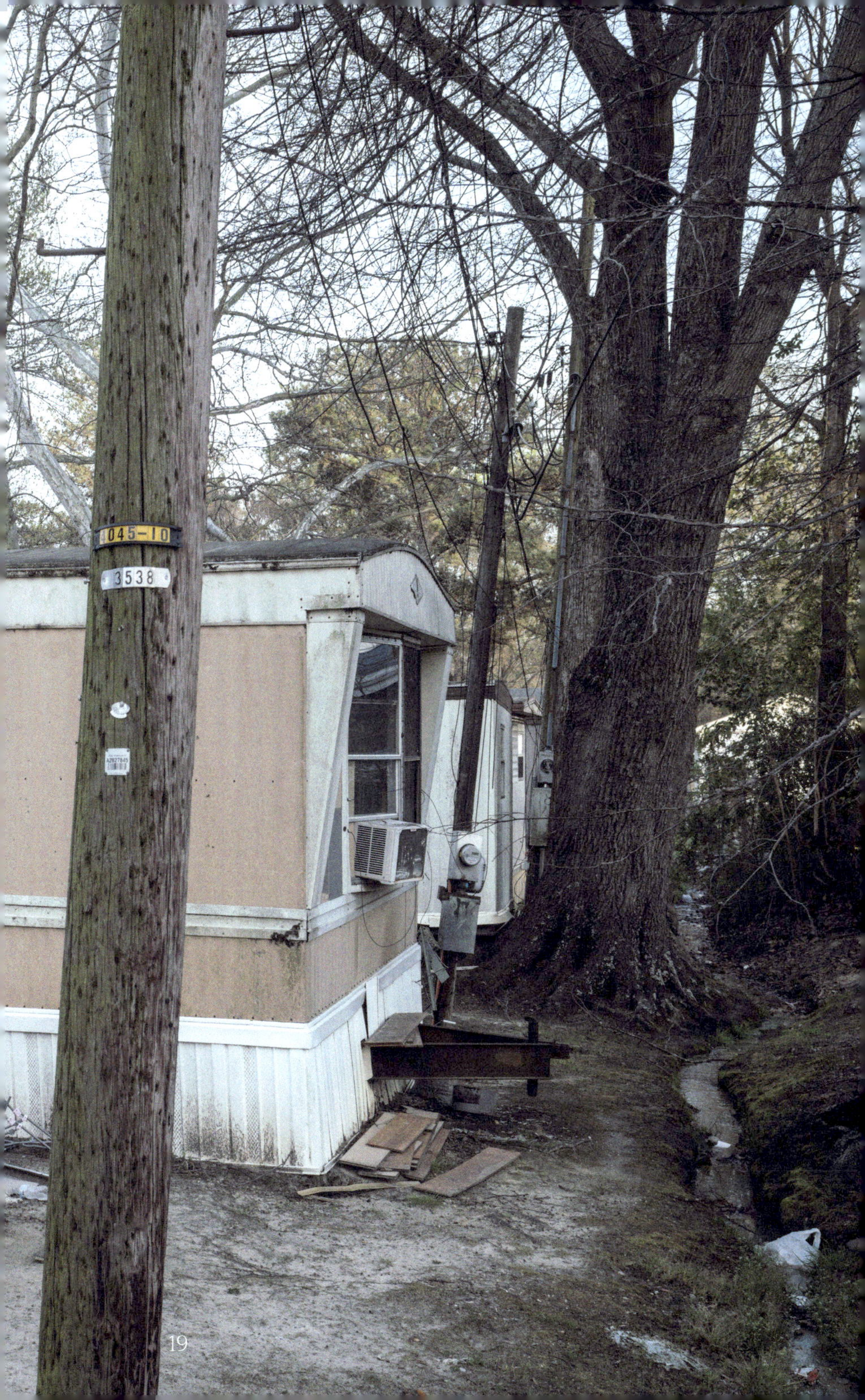
4045-10
3538

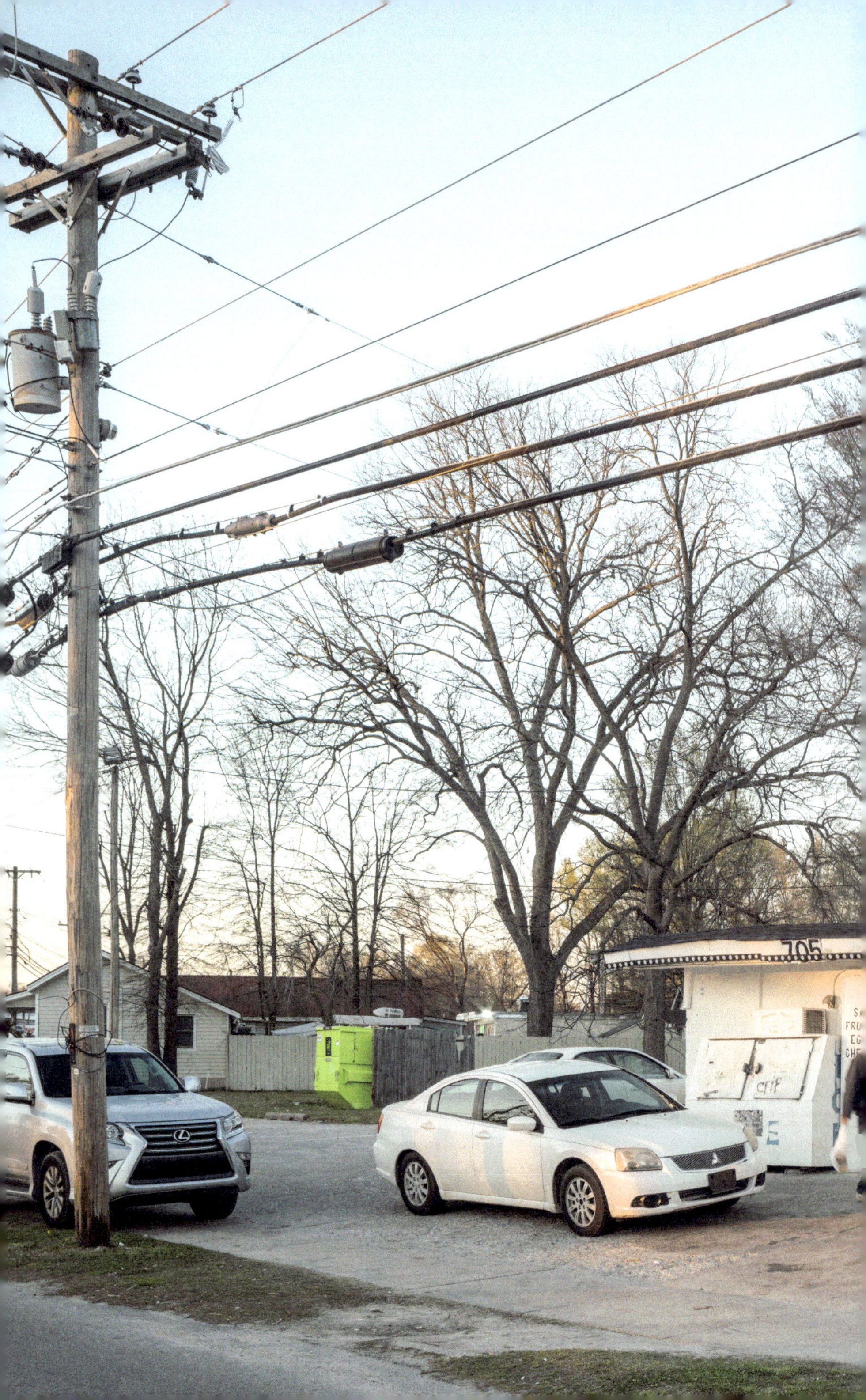
705

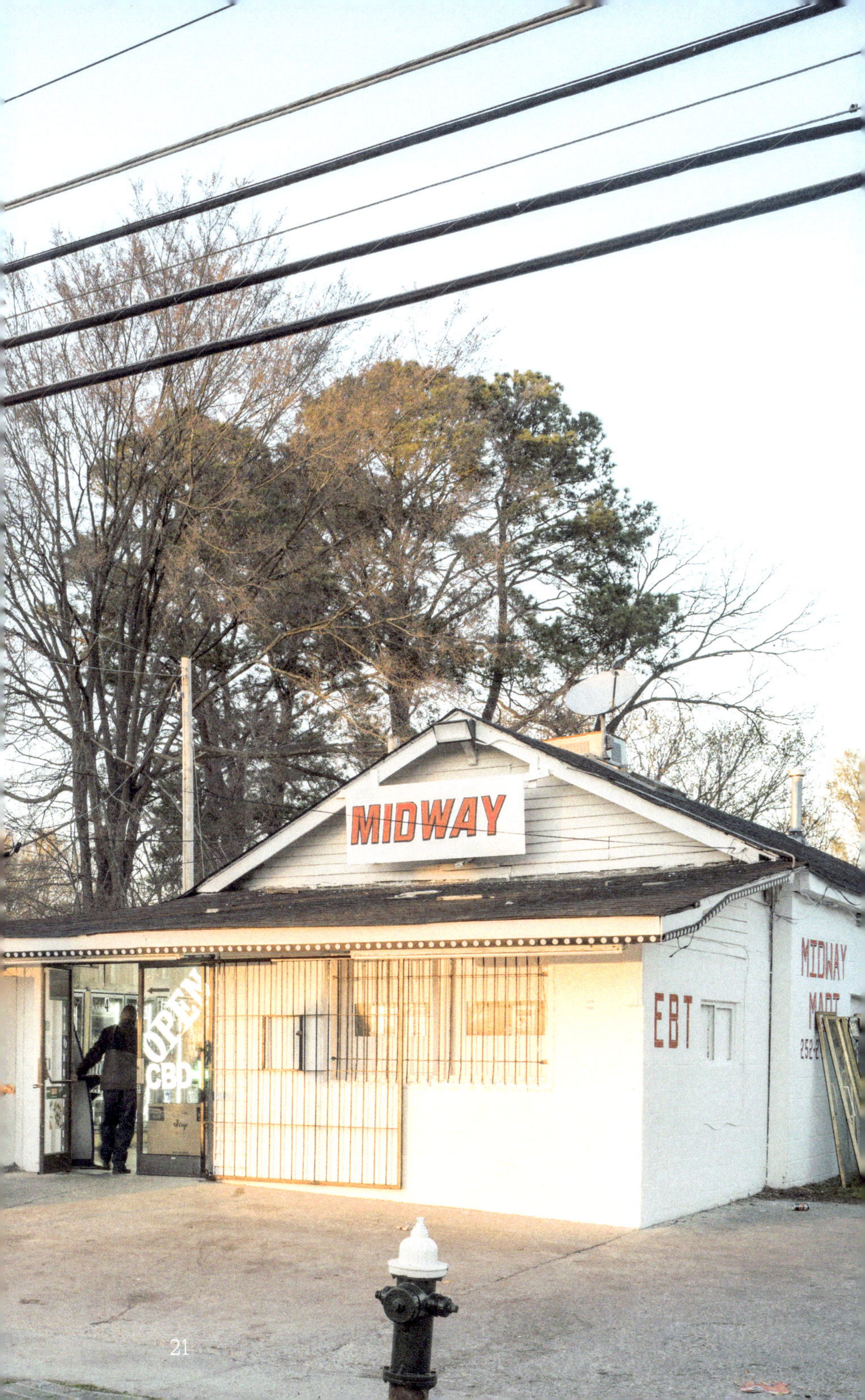
MIDWAY
OPEN
CBD
EBT
MIDWAY
MART

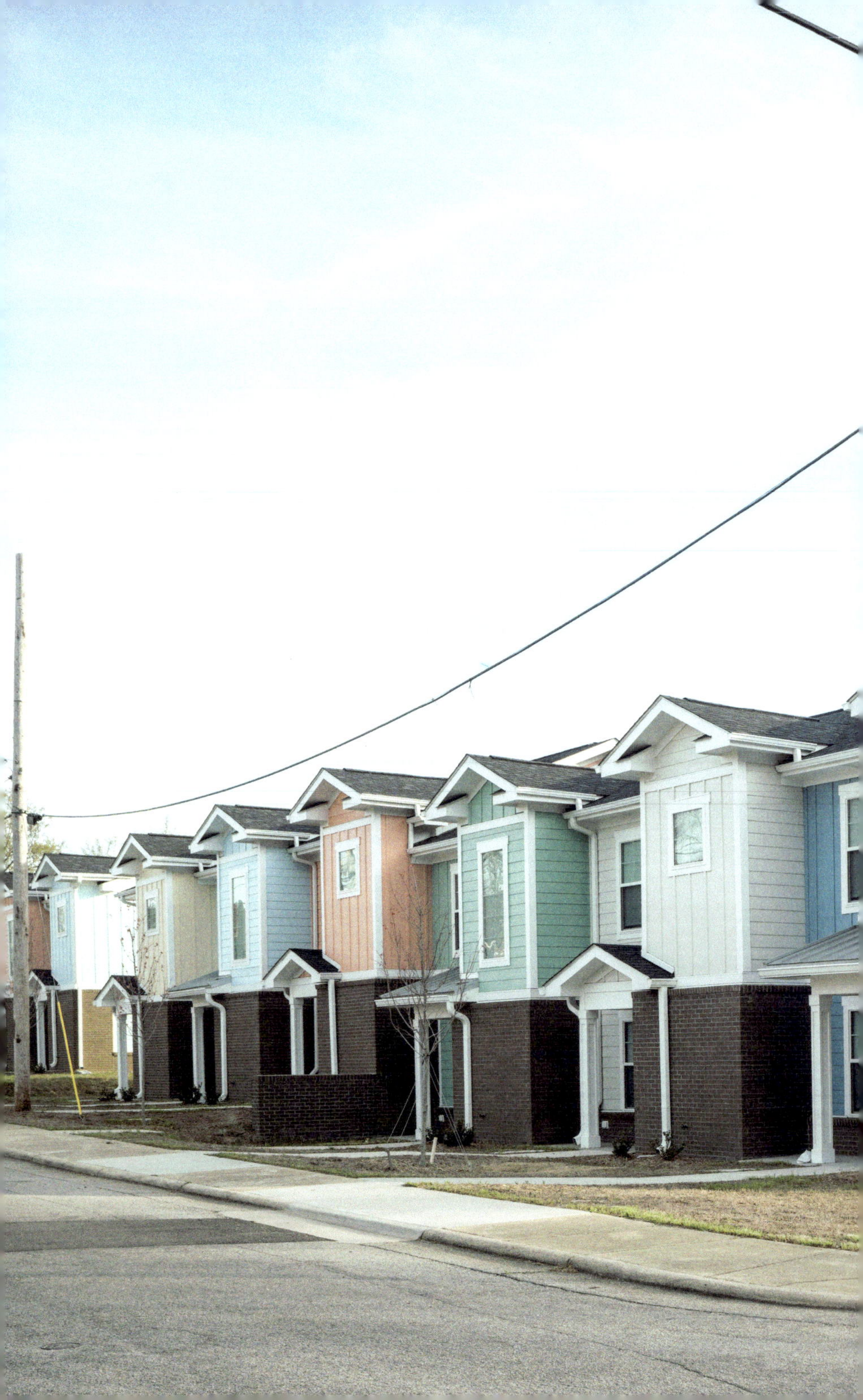

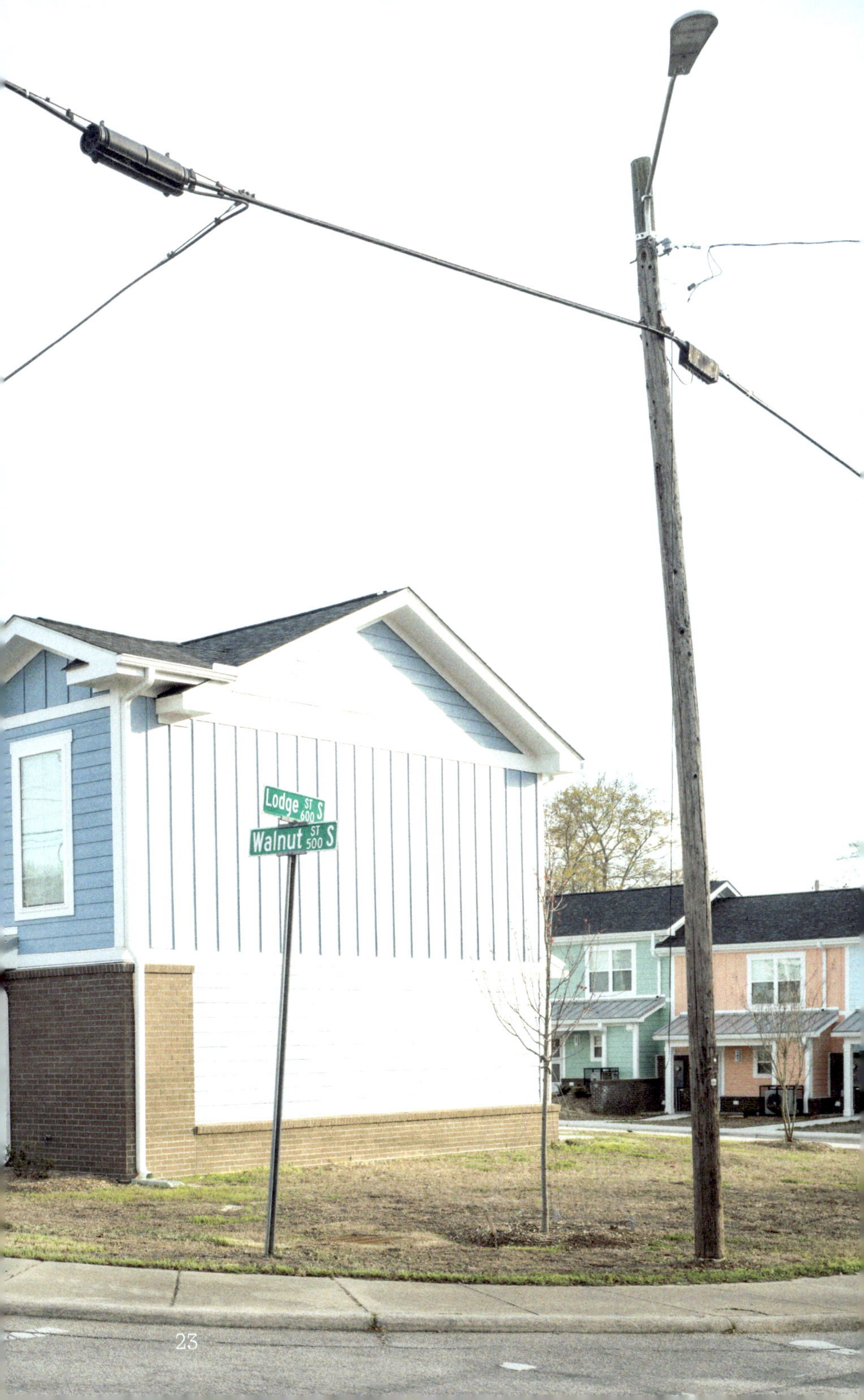
Lodge ST 600 S
Walnut ST 500 S

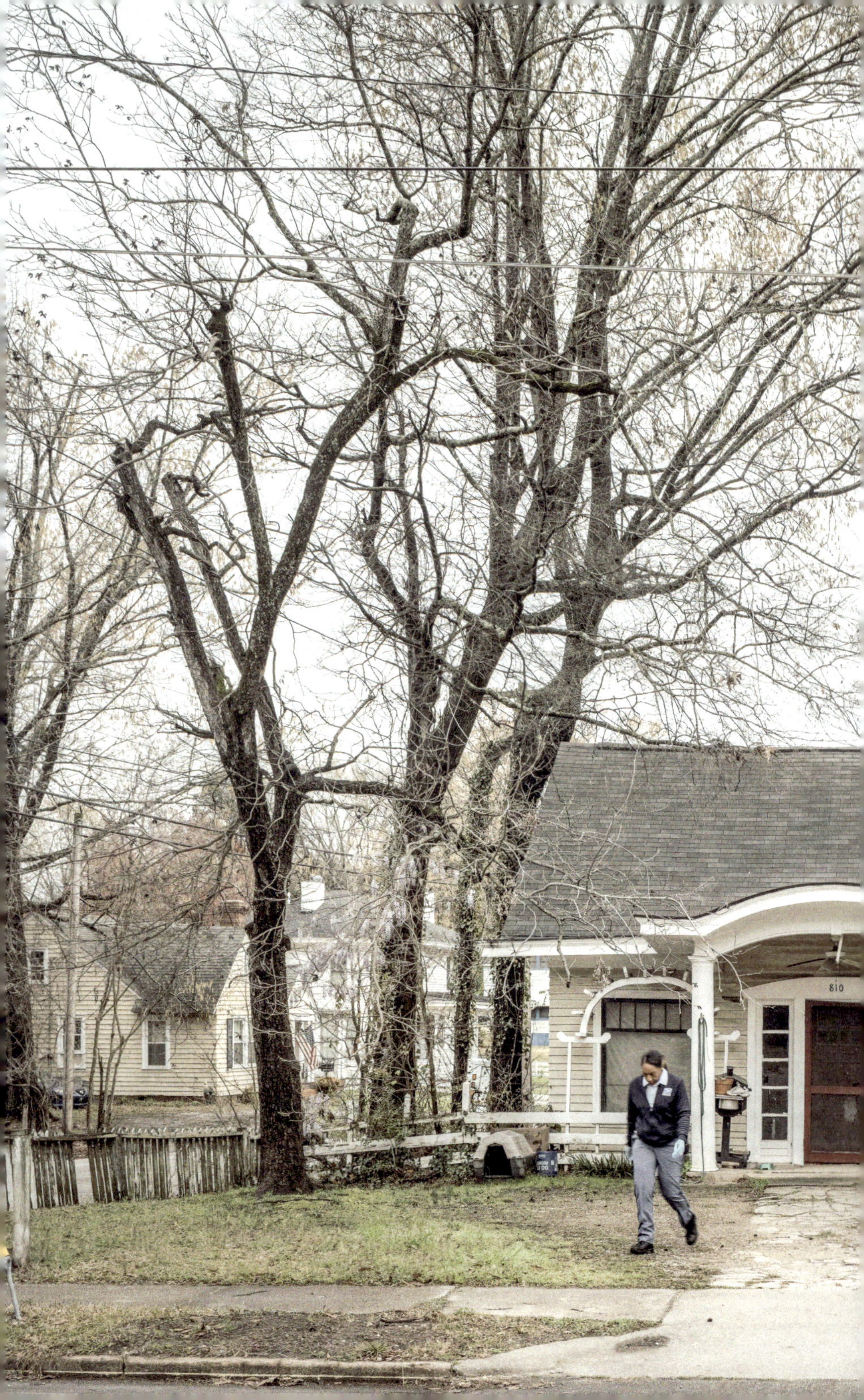
810

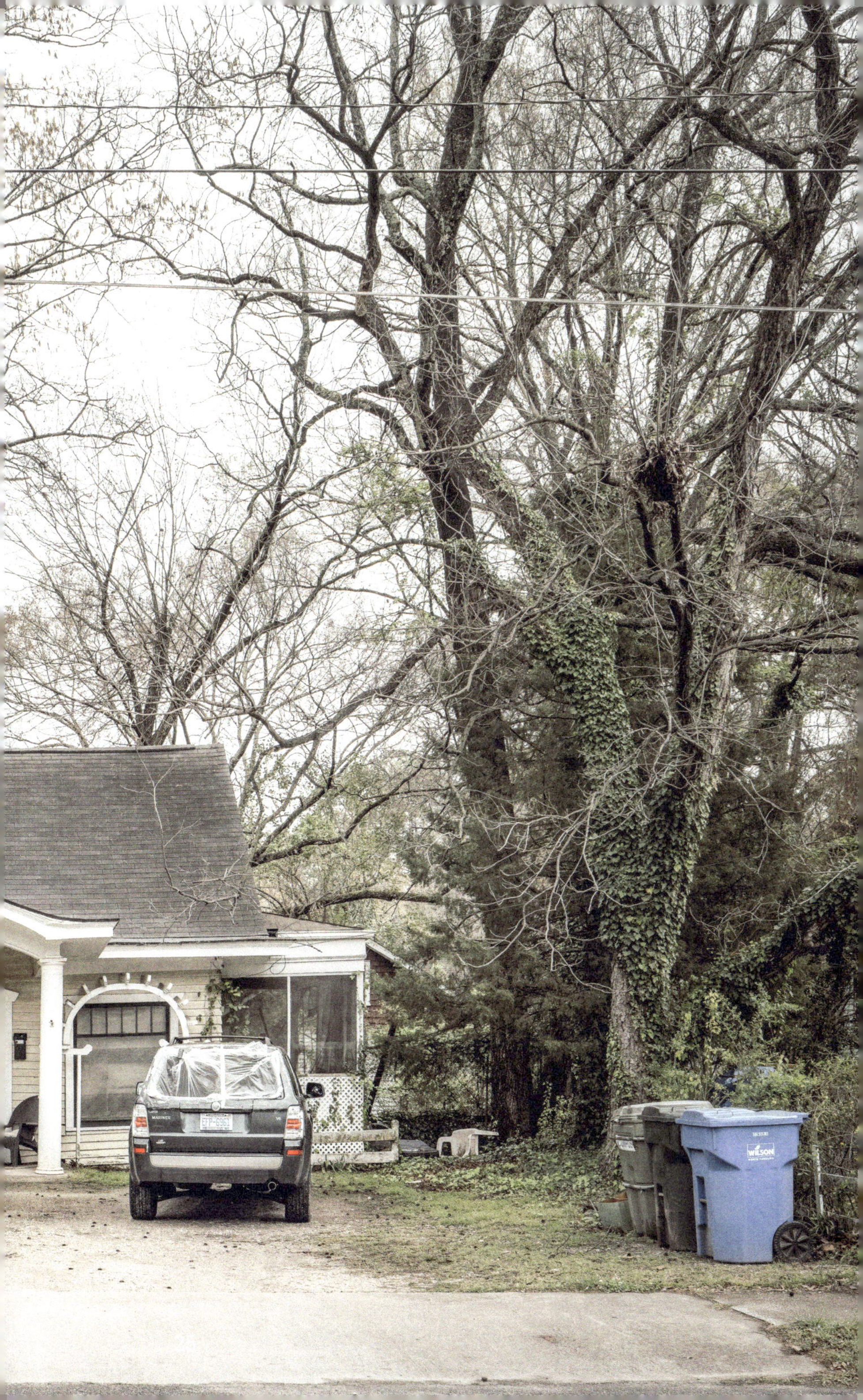
MARINER
EFP-6961
V6
WILSON

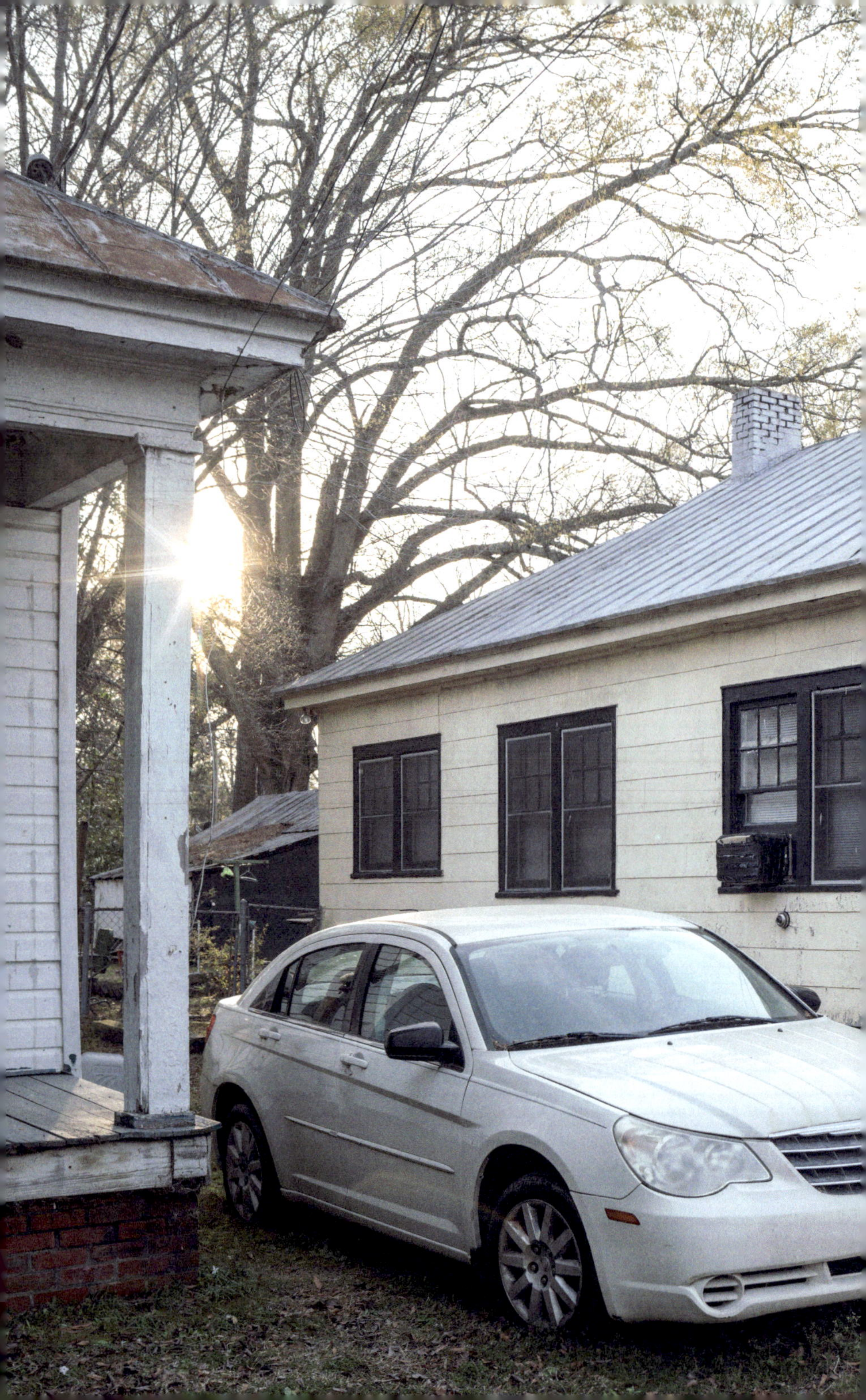

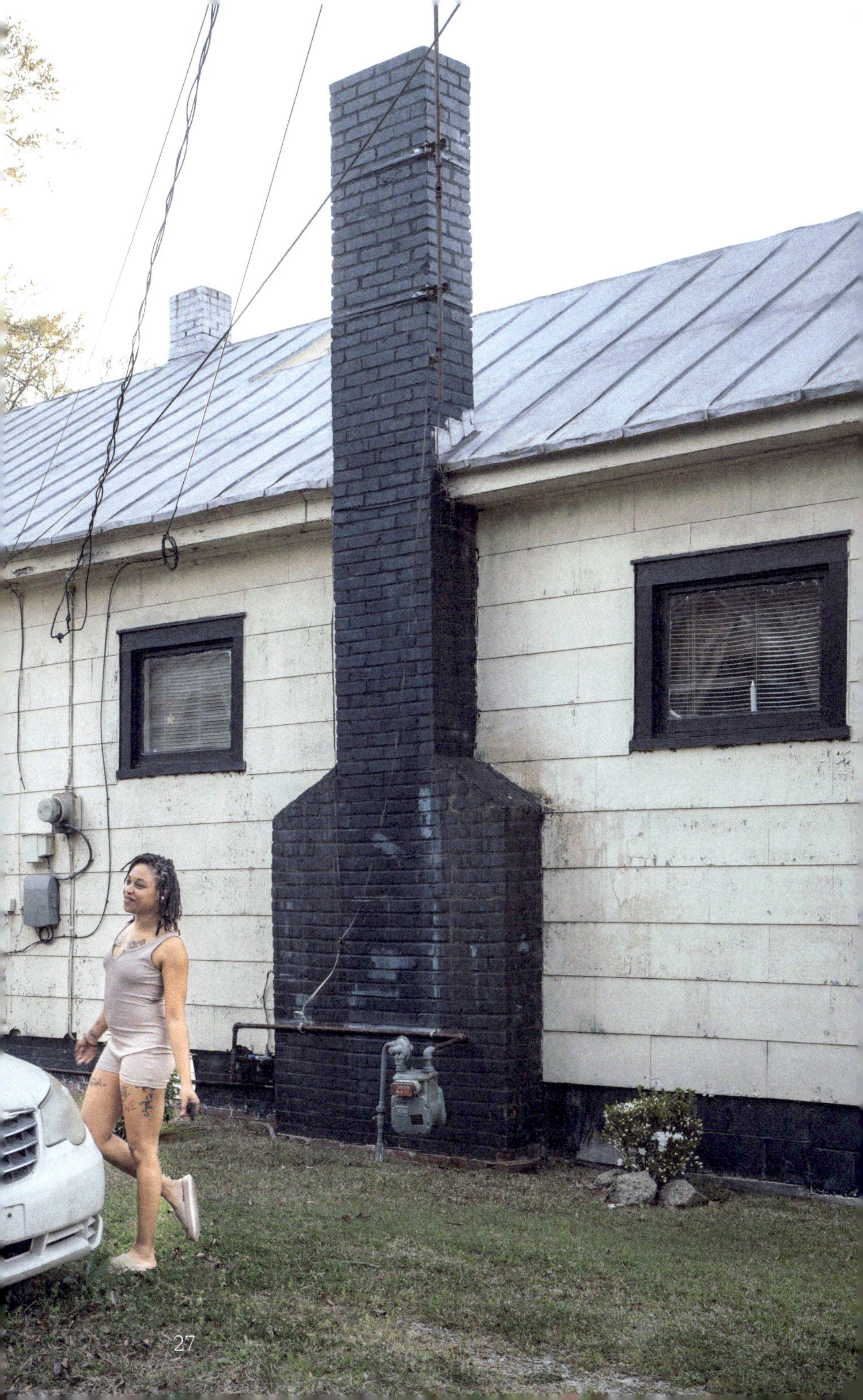

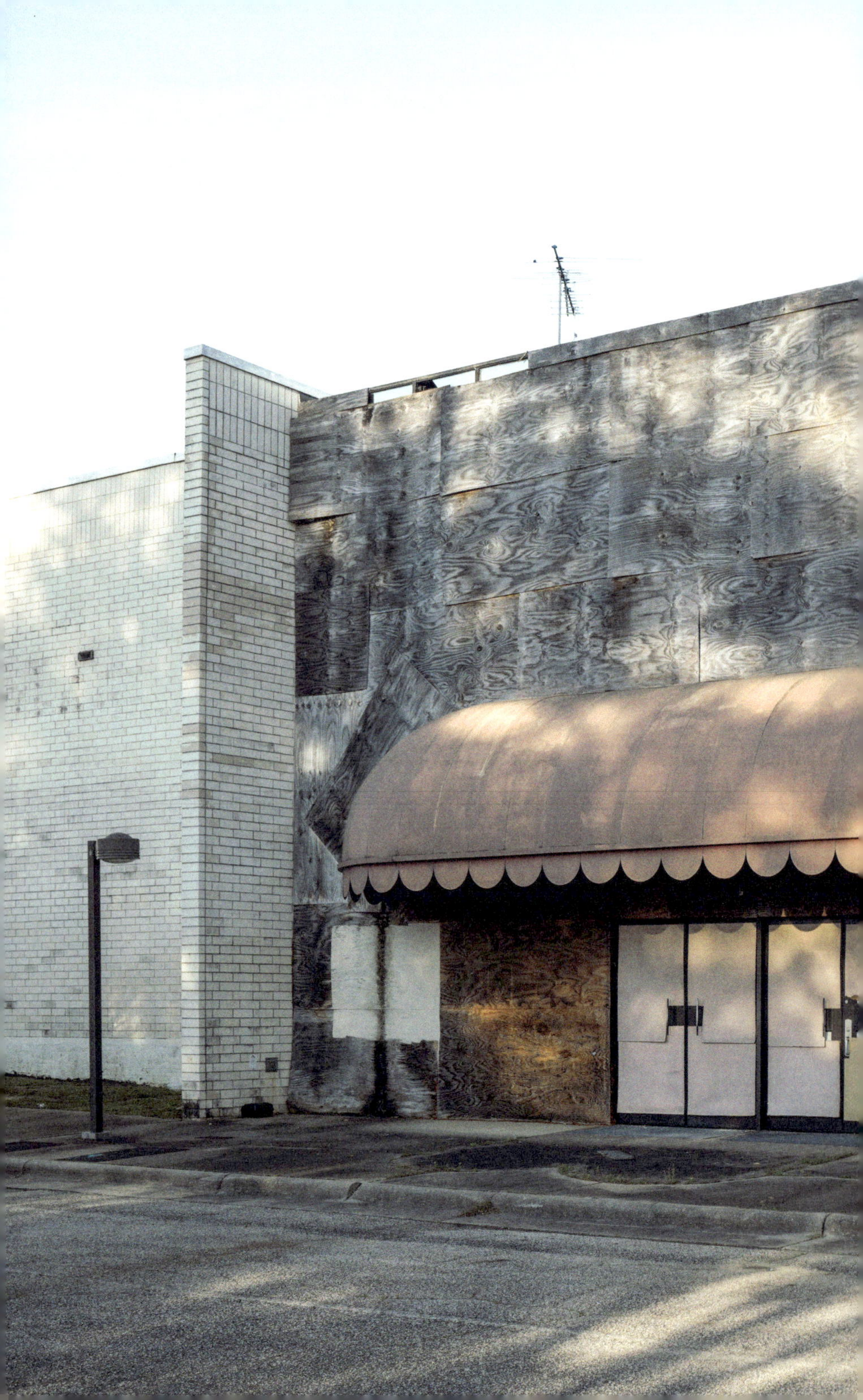

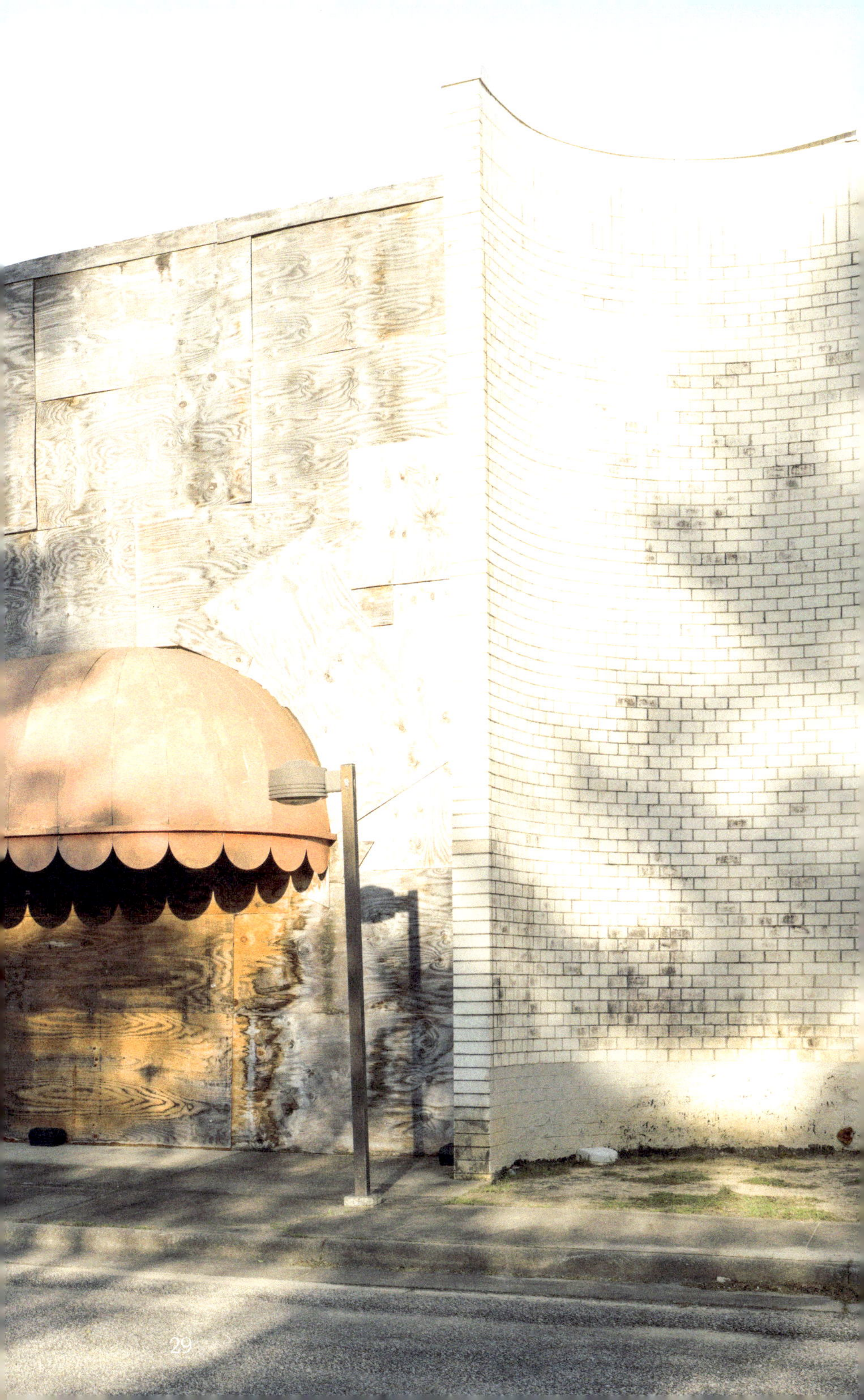

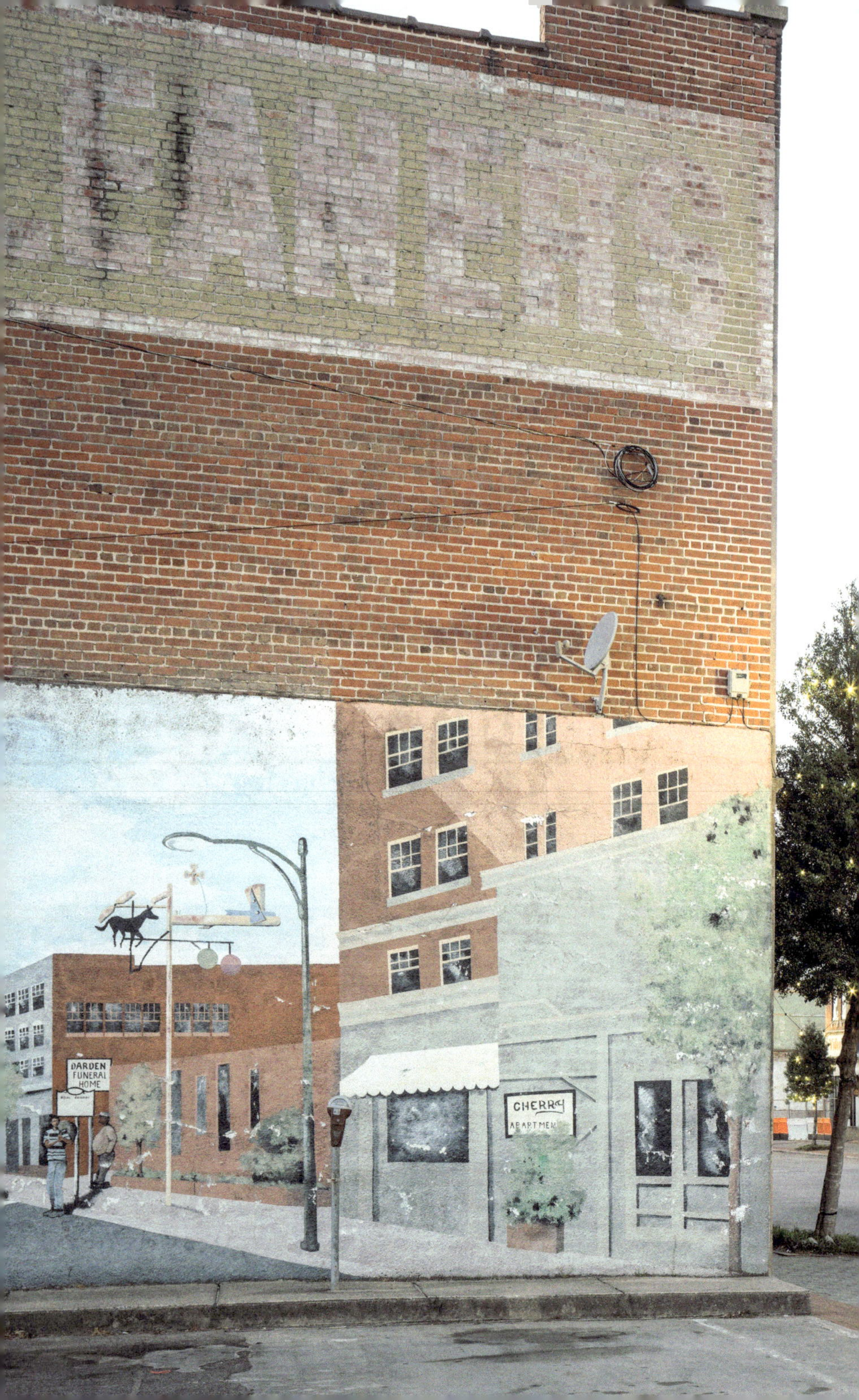
DARDEN
FUNERAL
HOME
CHERRY
APARTMEN

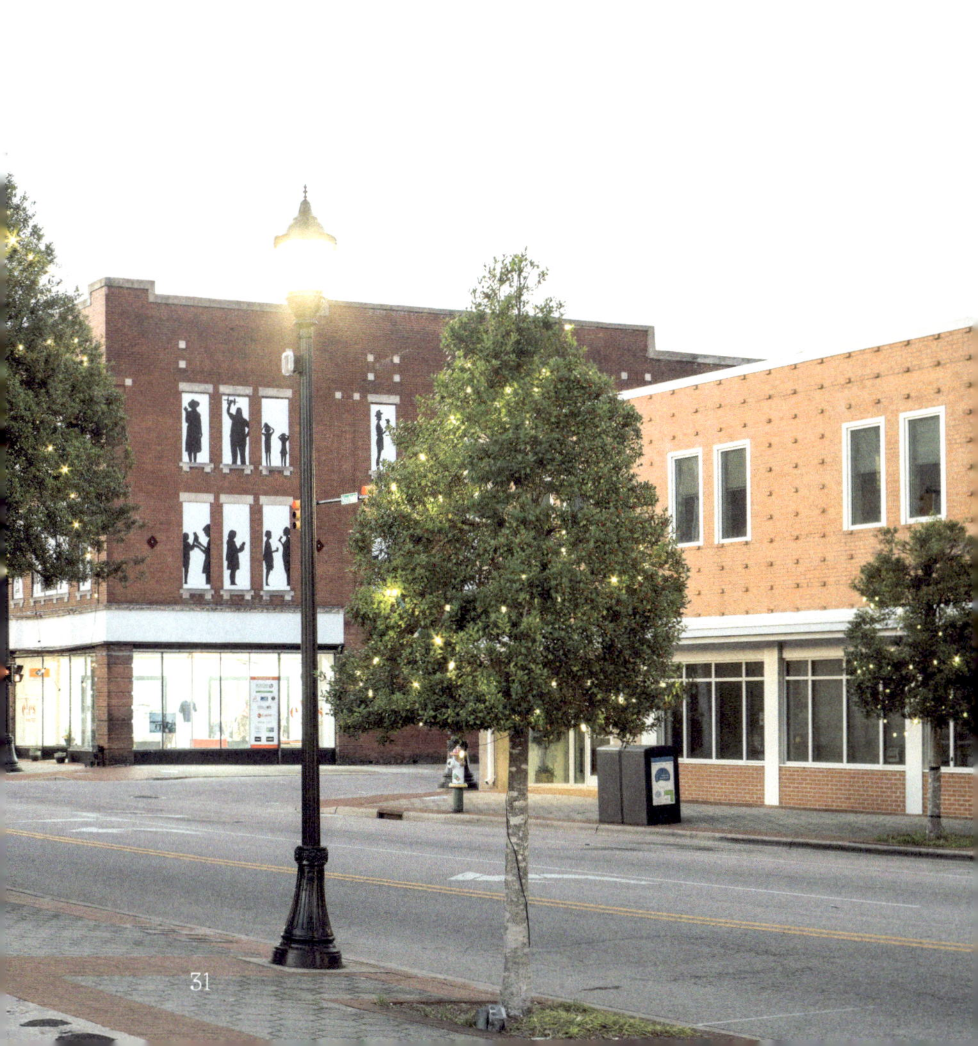

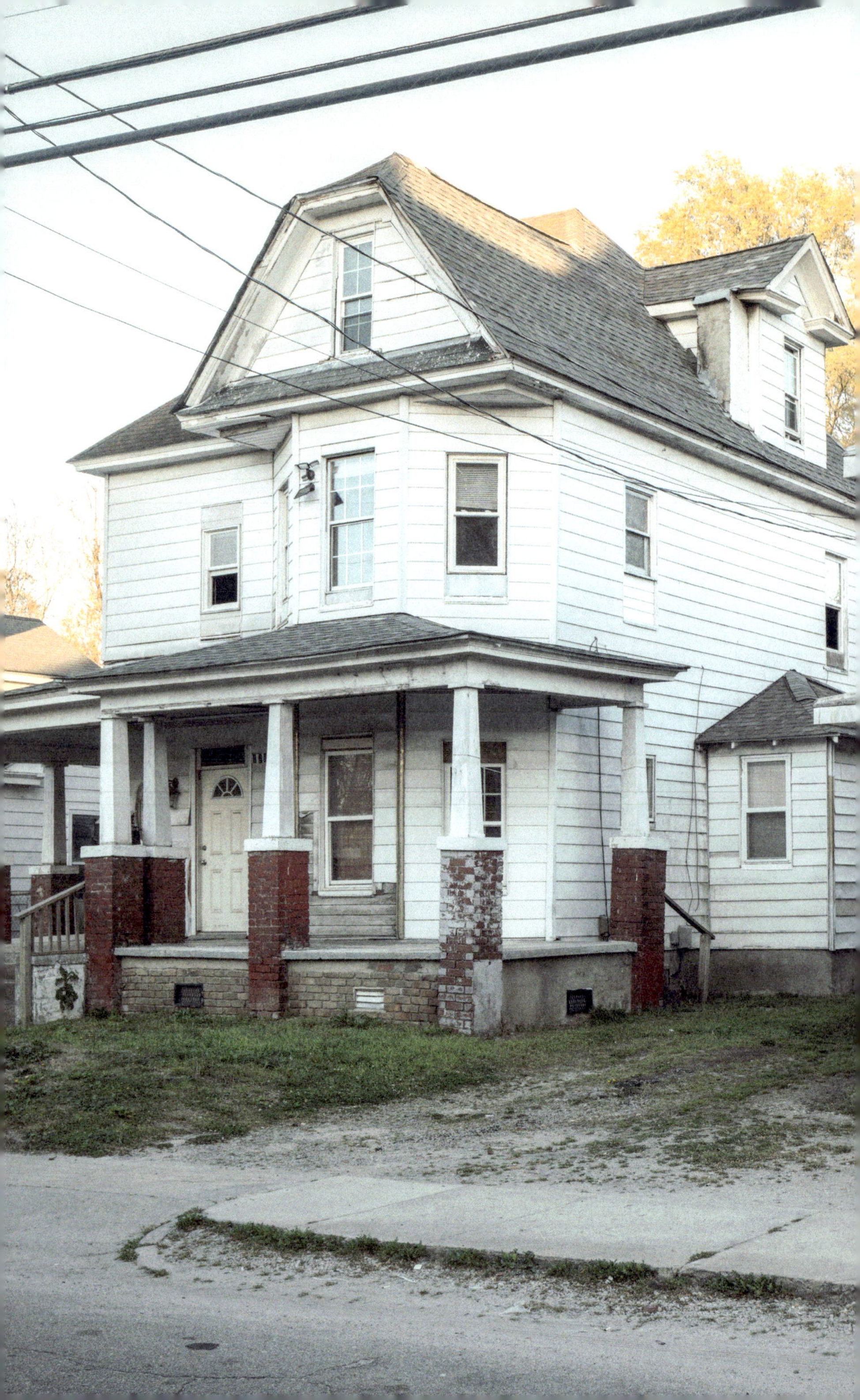

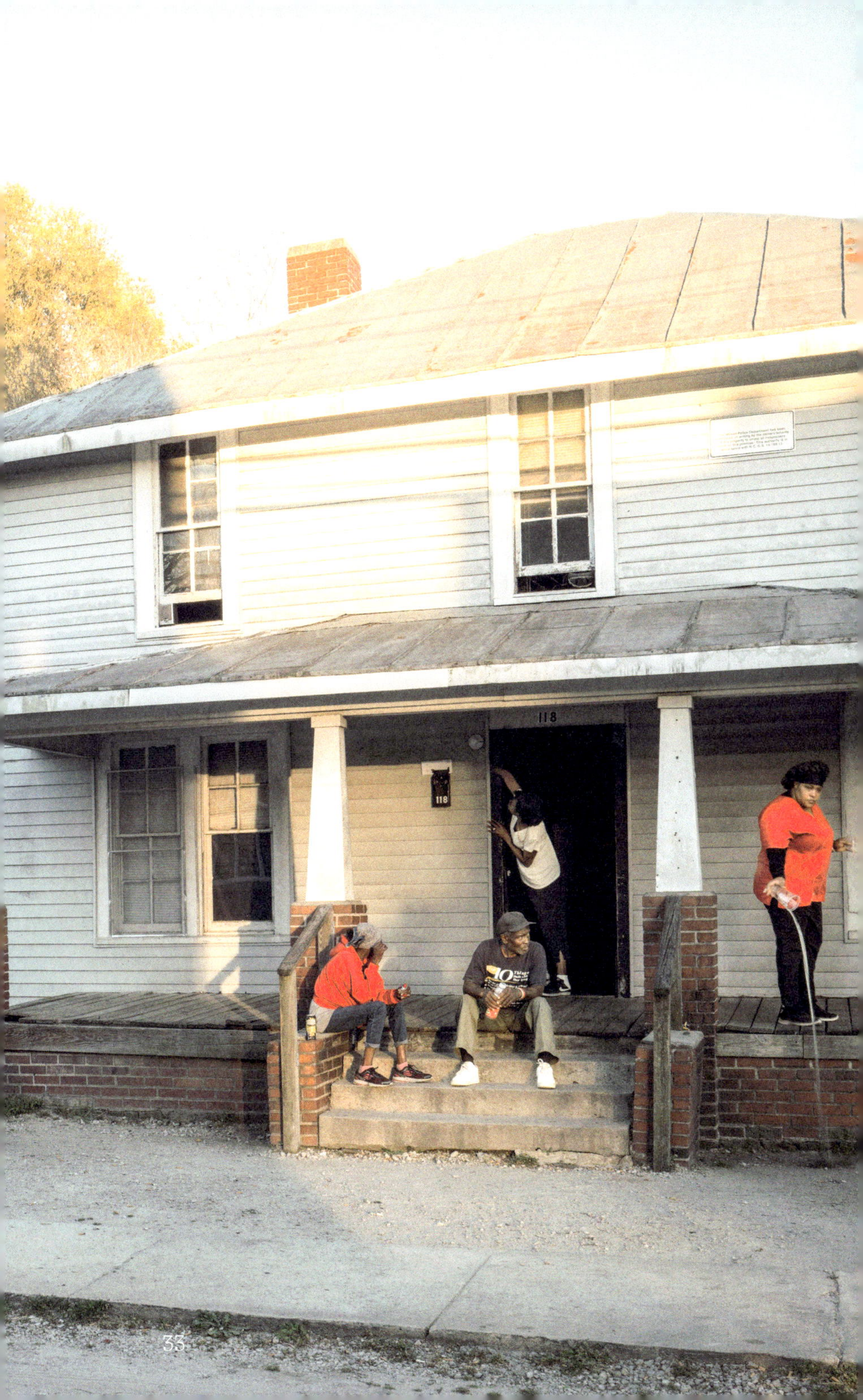
118
118

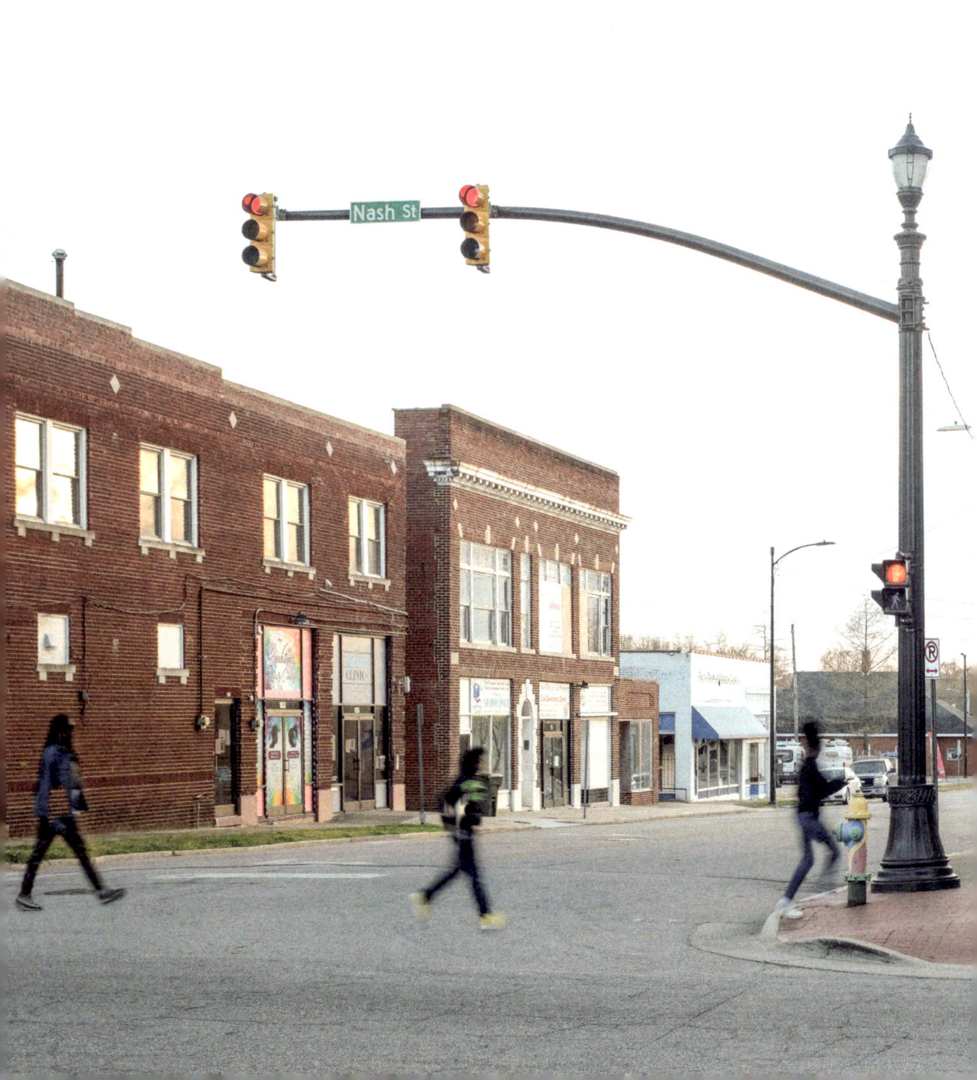
Nash St

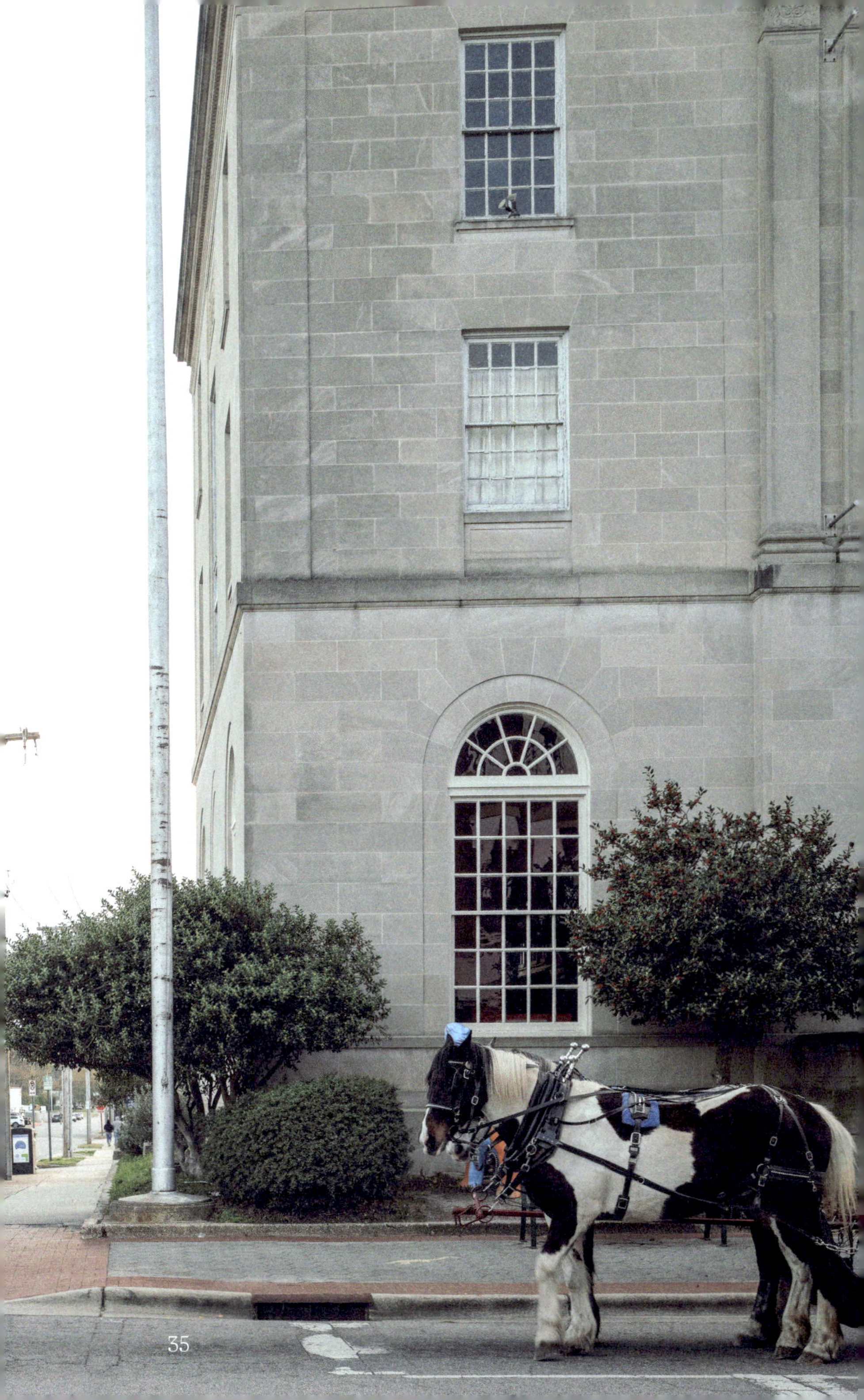

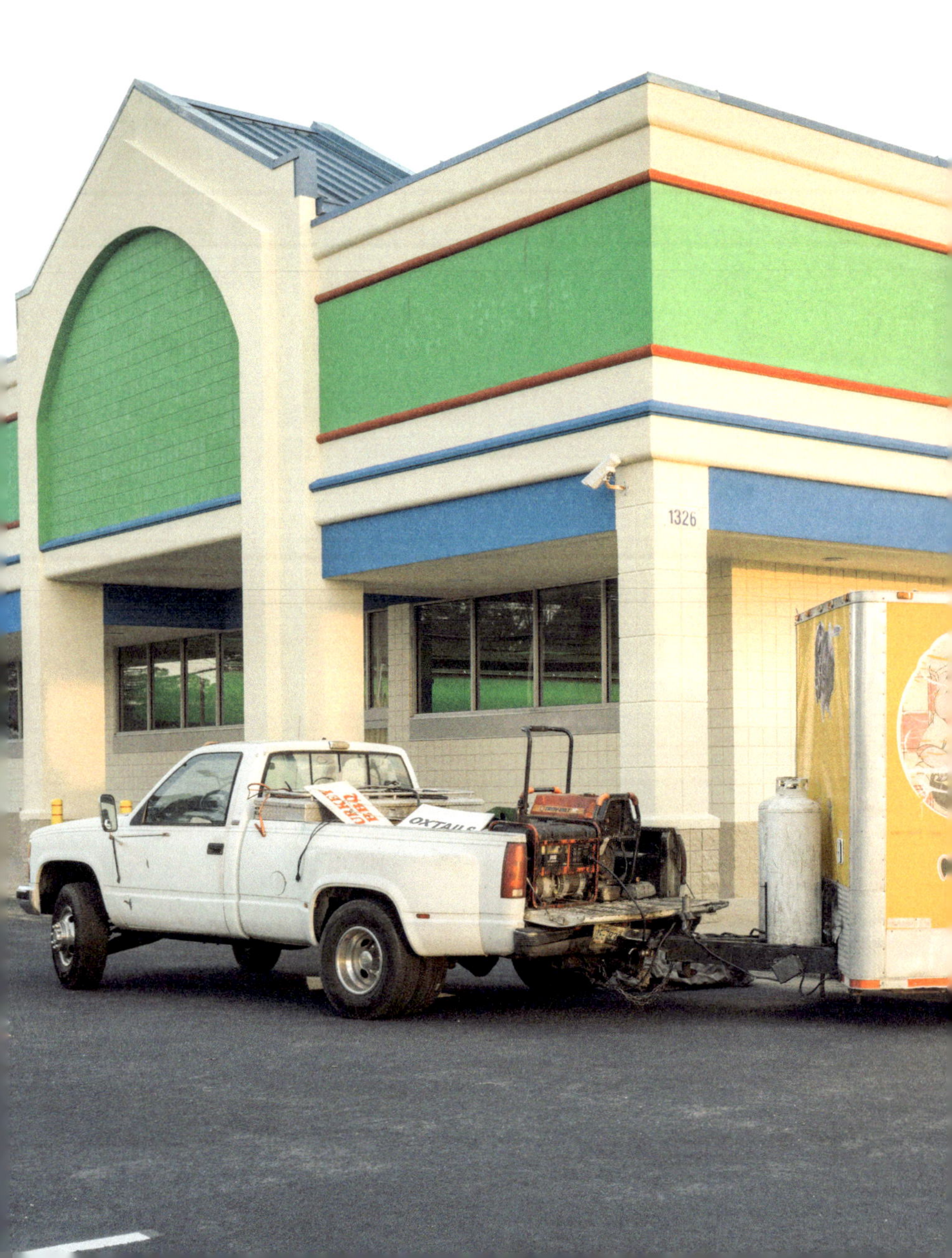
1326
OXTAILS

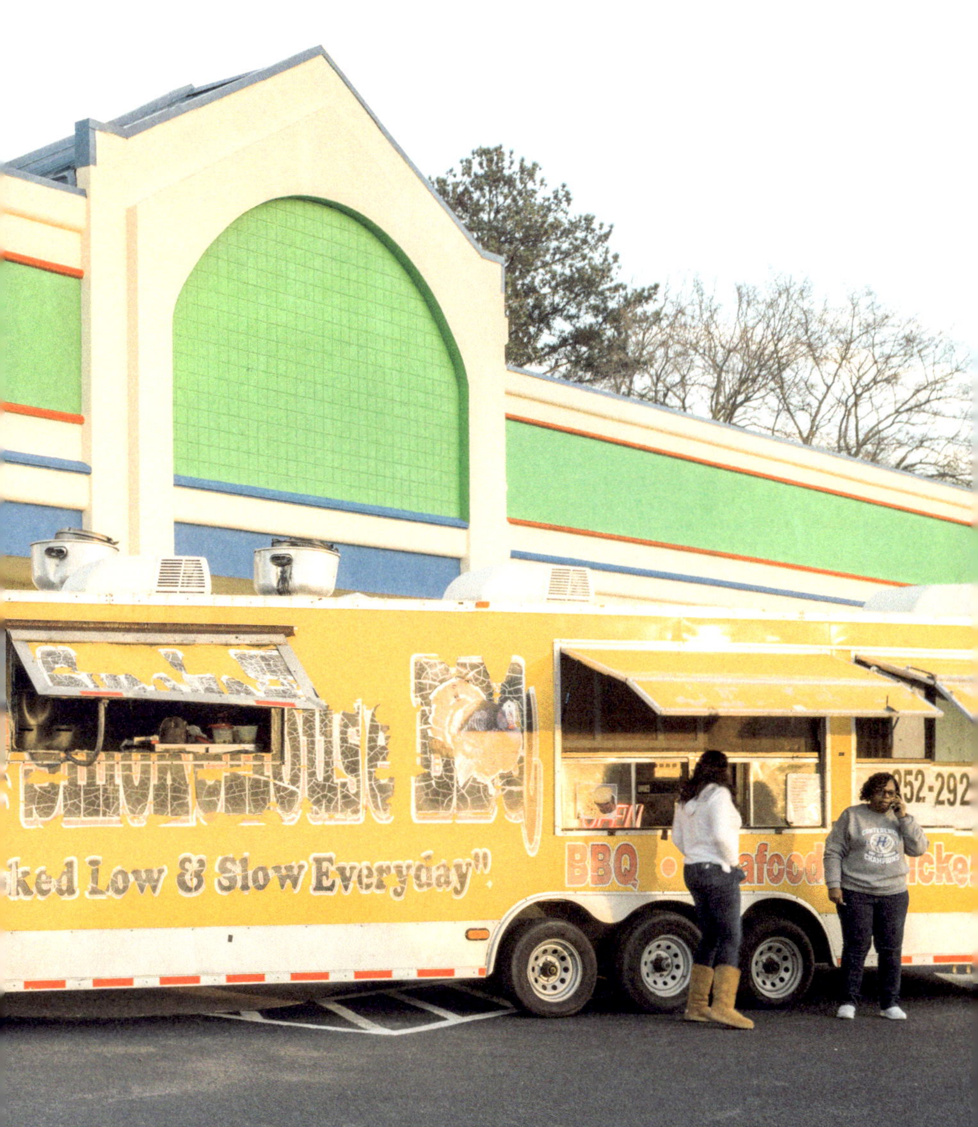
ked Low & Slow Everyday".
BBQ

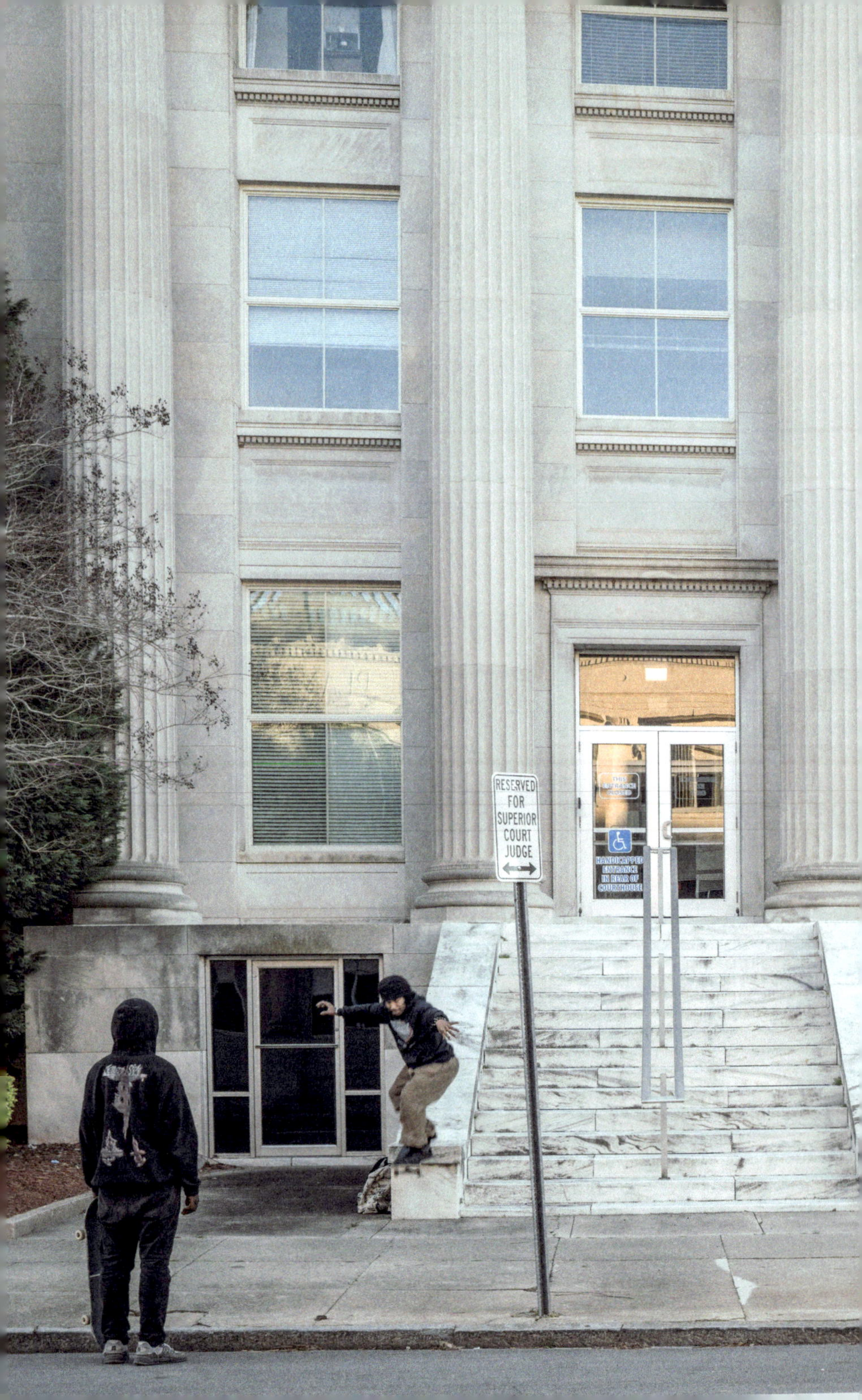
RESERVED FOR SUPERIOR COURT JUDGE
HANDICAPPED ENTRANCE IN REAR OF COURTHOUSE

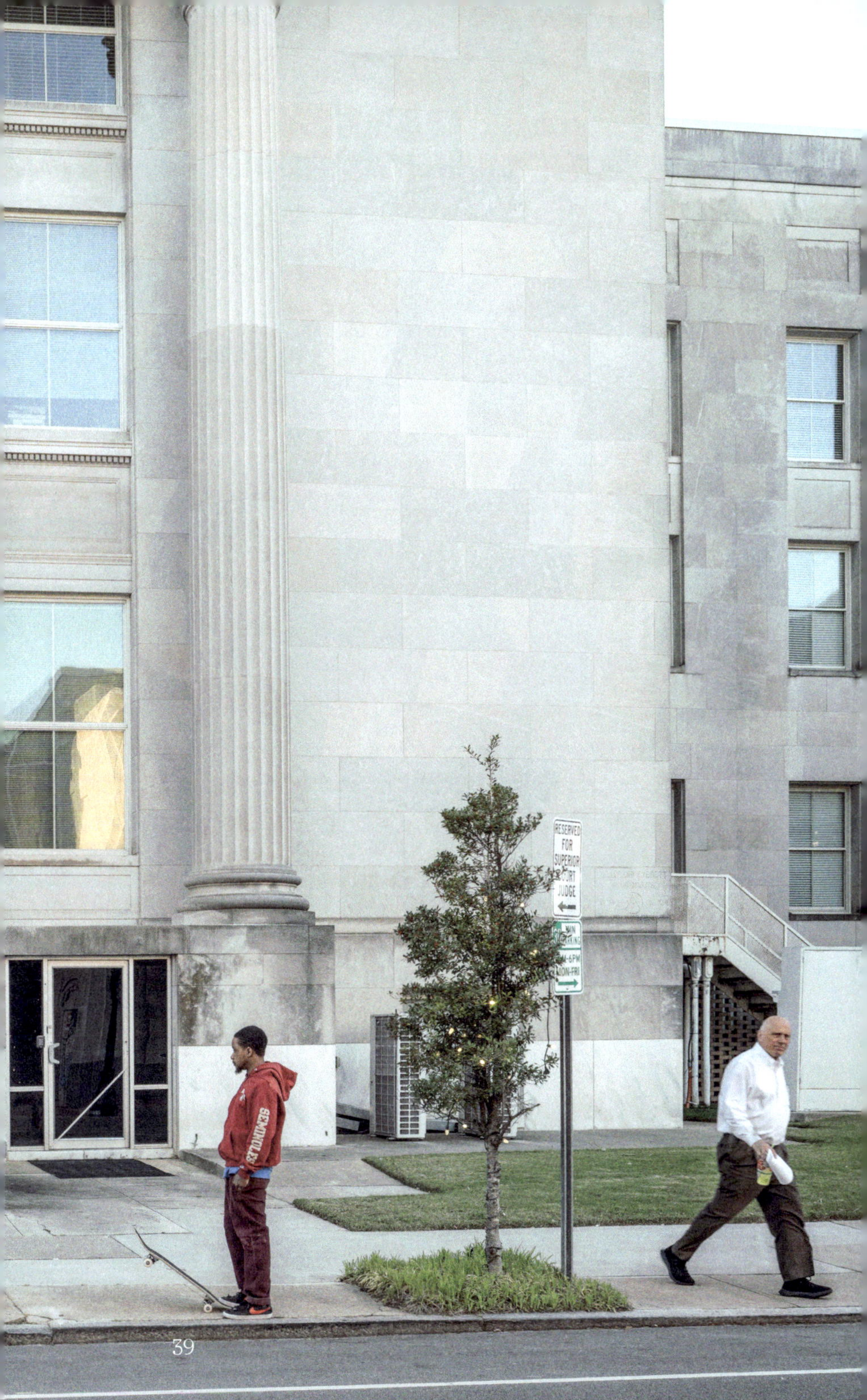
RESERVED
FOR
SUPERIOR
JUDGE
MON-FRI
SEMINOLES

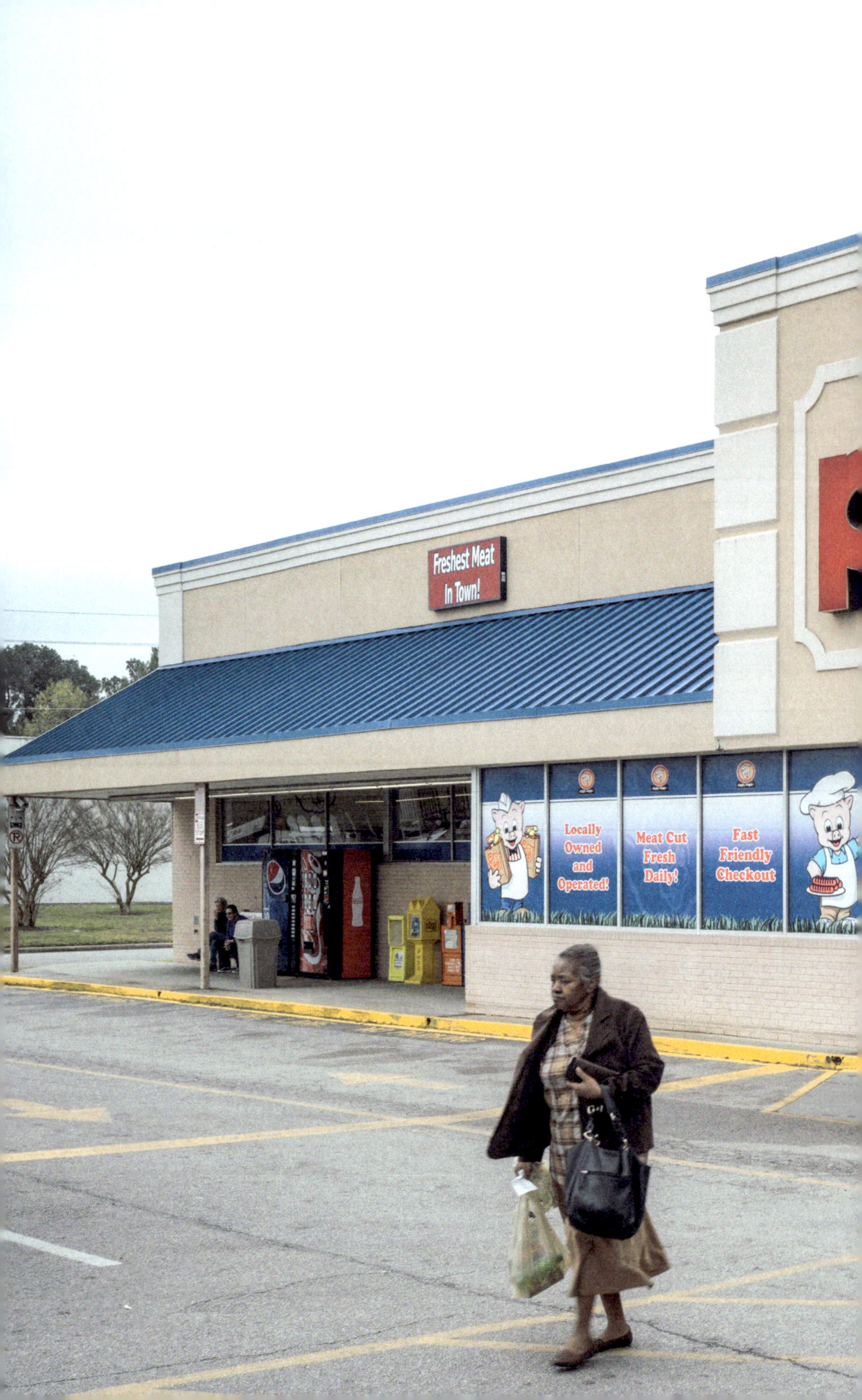
Freshest Meat
In Town!
Locally
Owned
and
Operated!
Meat Cut
Fresh
Daily!
Fast
Friendly
Checkout

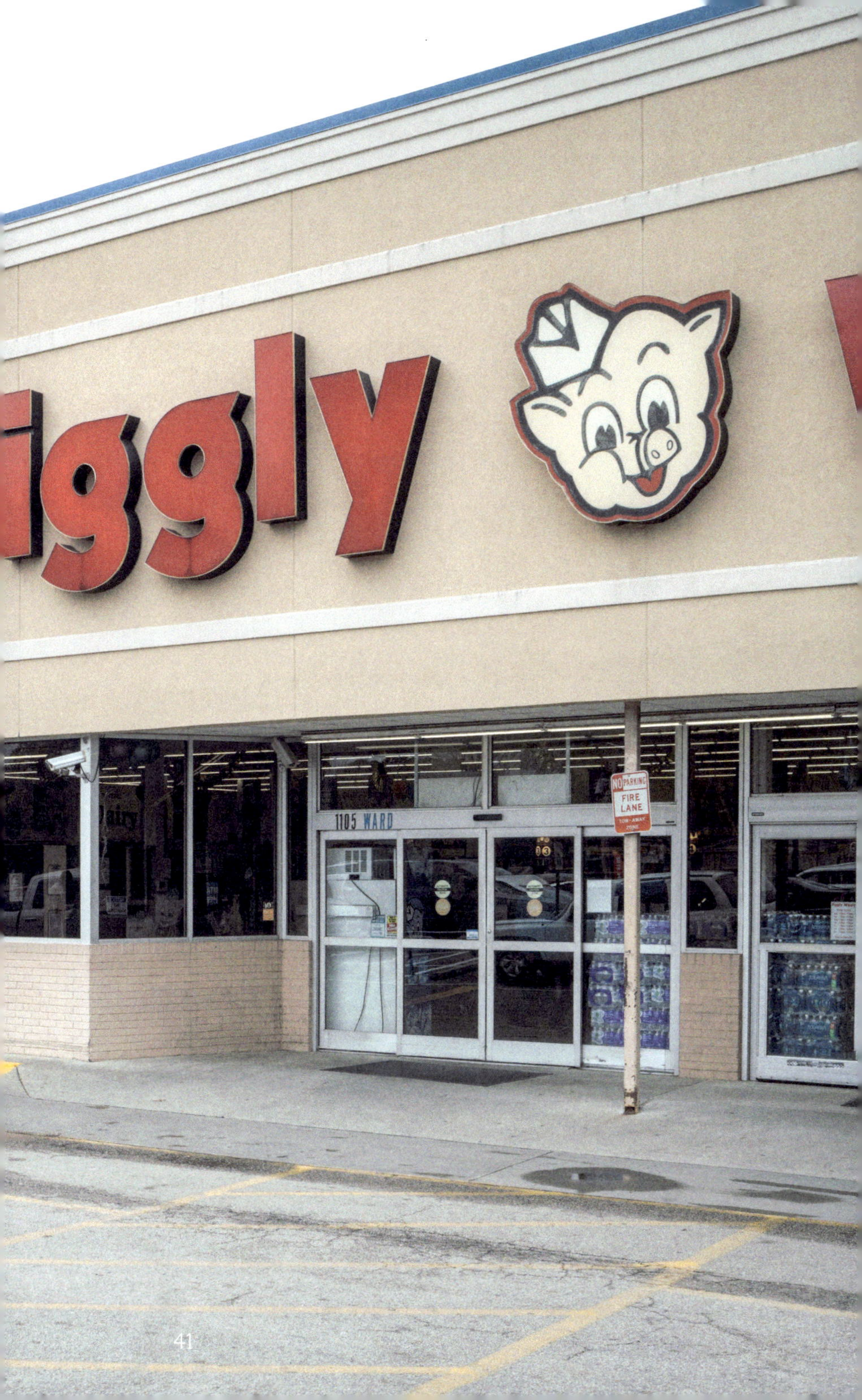
iggly
1105 WARD
NO PARKING
FIRE
LANE
TOW-AWAY
ZONE

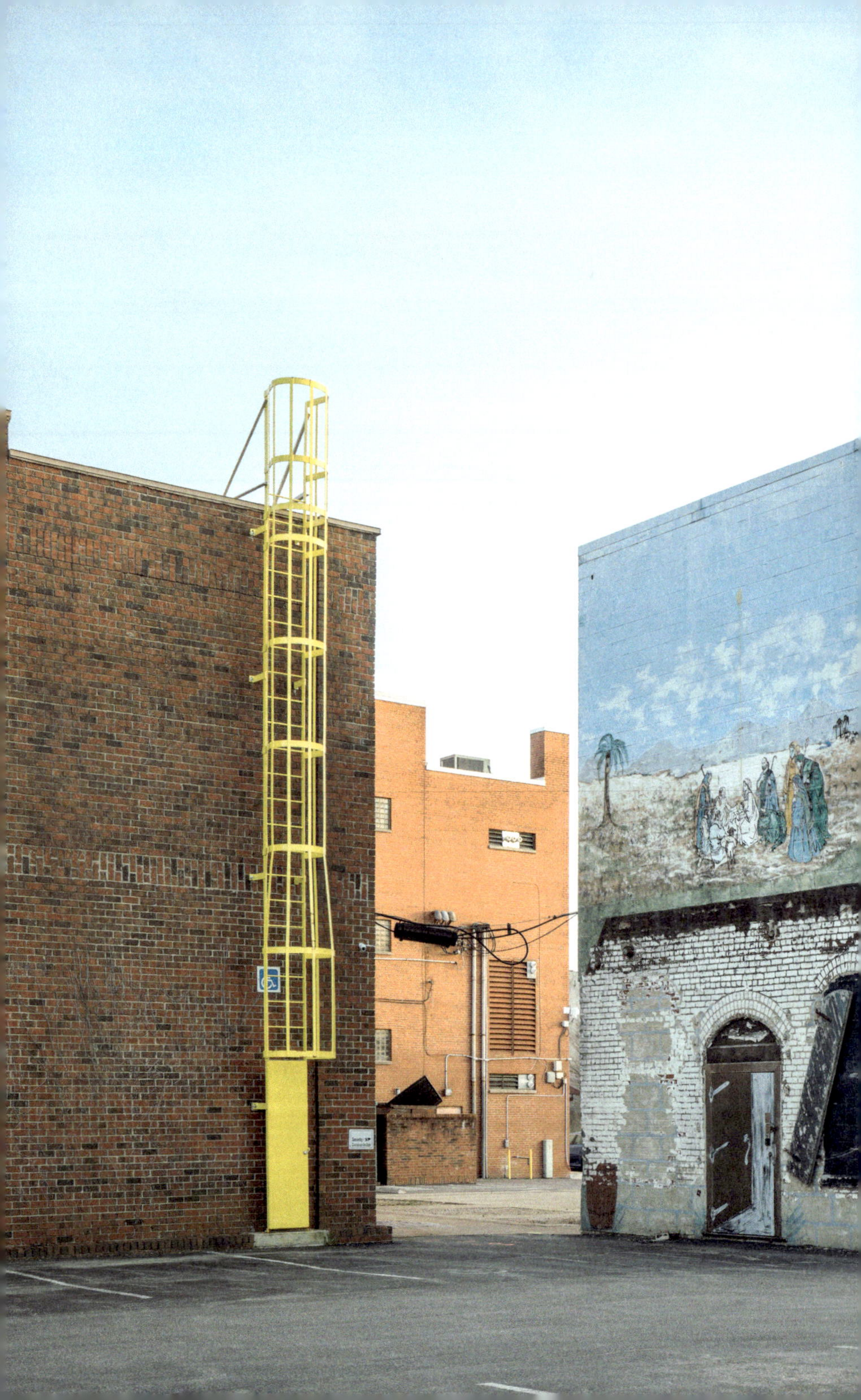

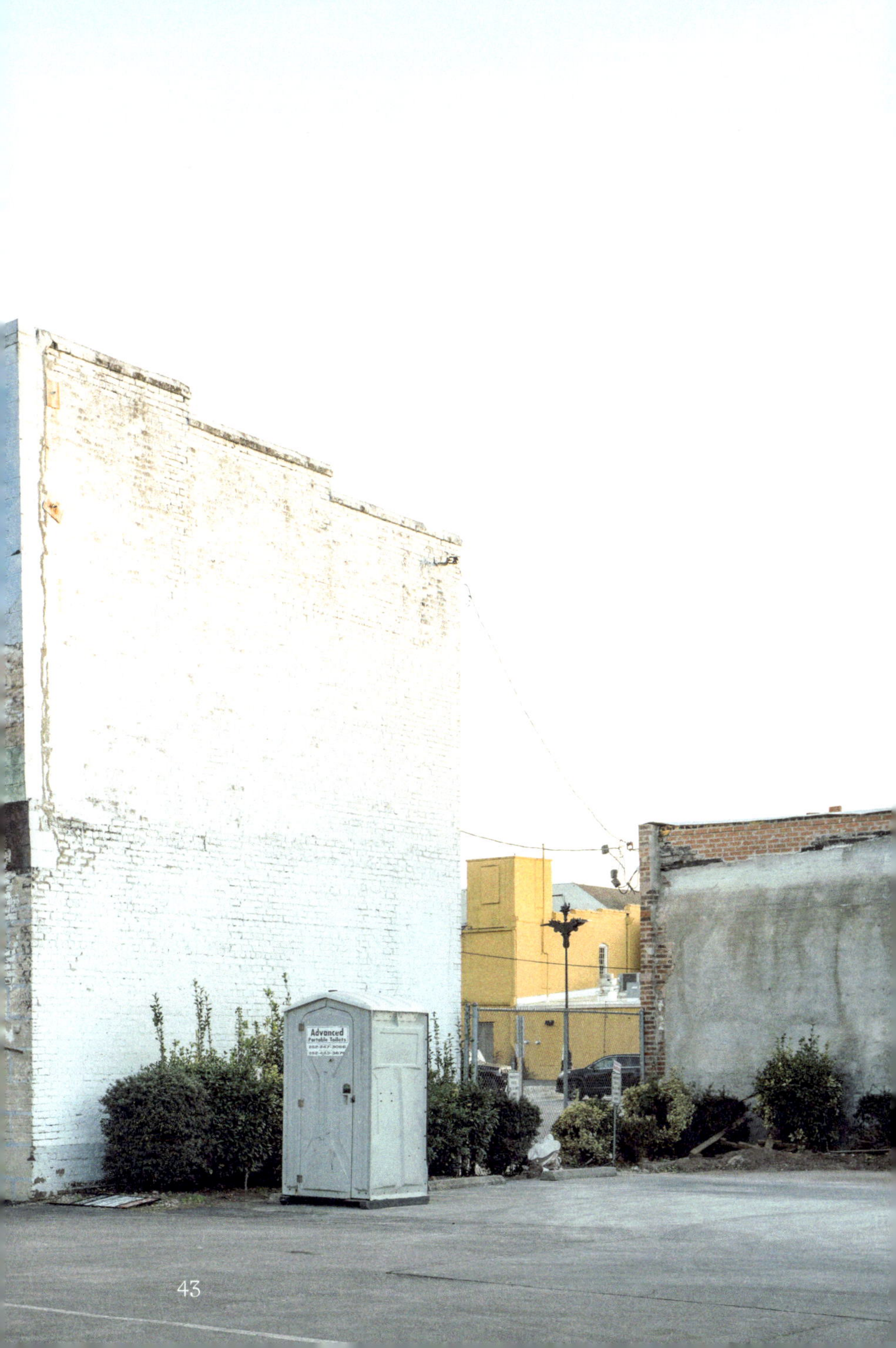
Advanced
Portable Toilets

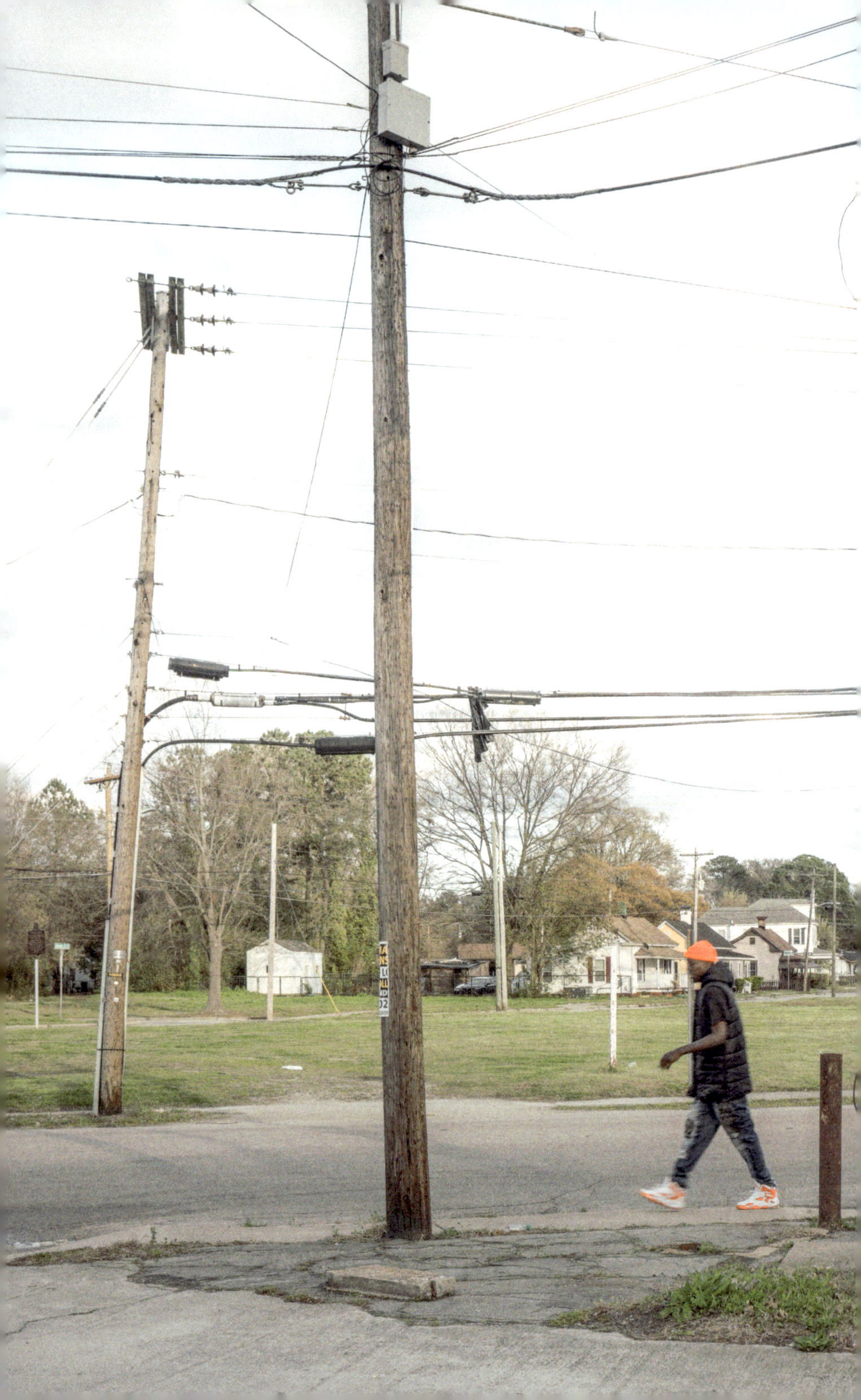

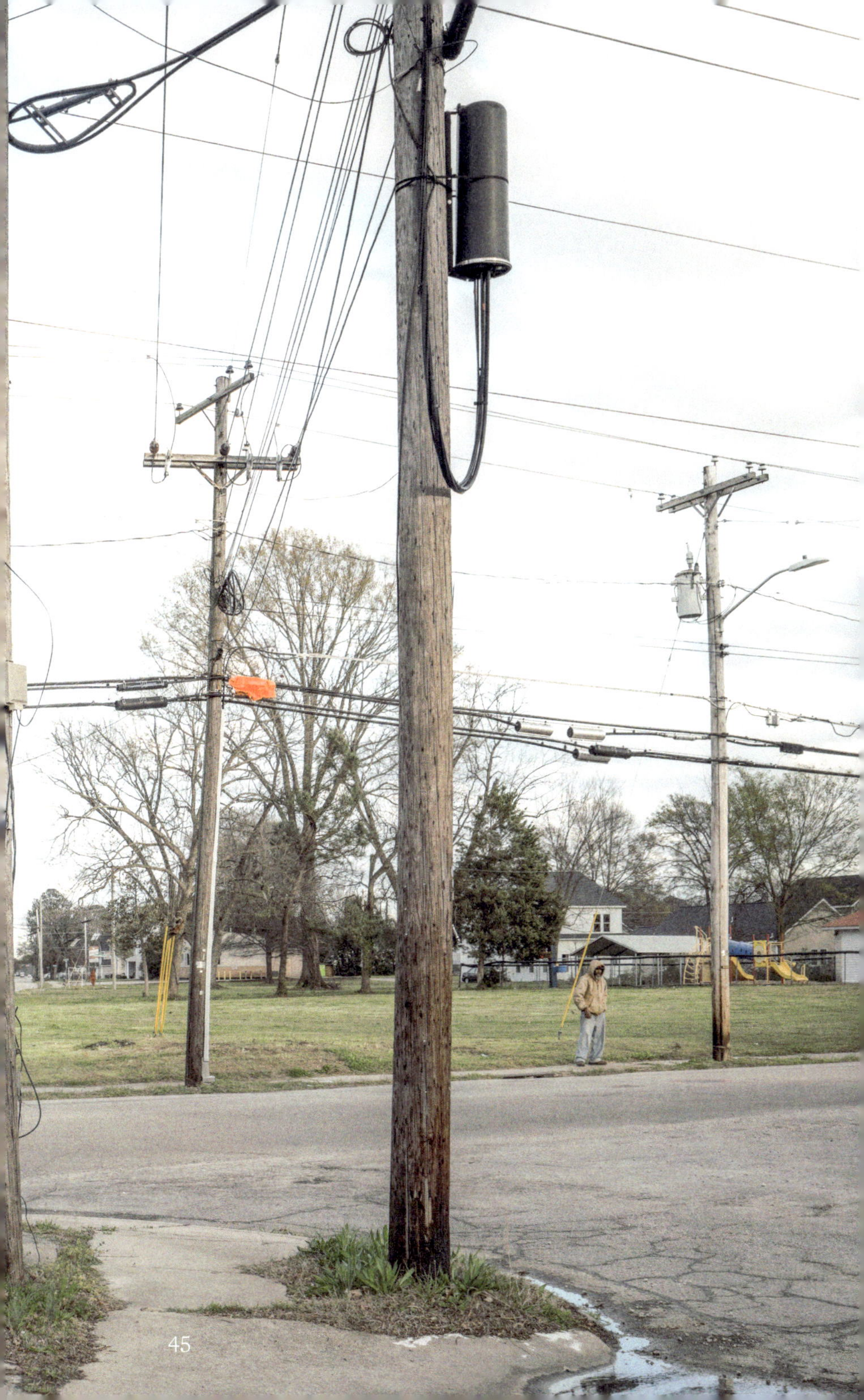

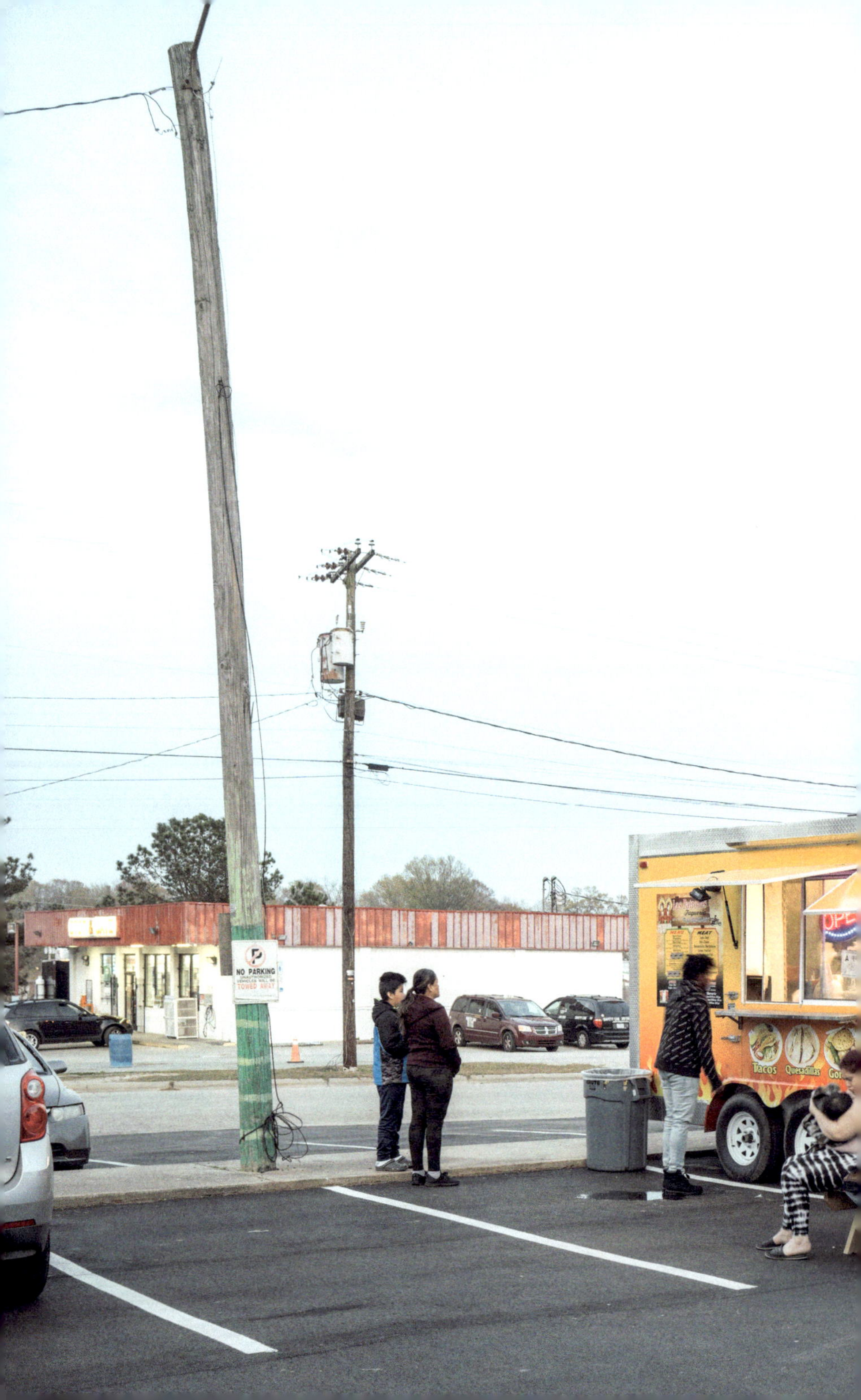
NO PARKING
UNAUTHORIZED
VEHICLES WILL BE
TOWED AWAY
Tacos
Quesadillas

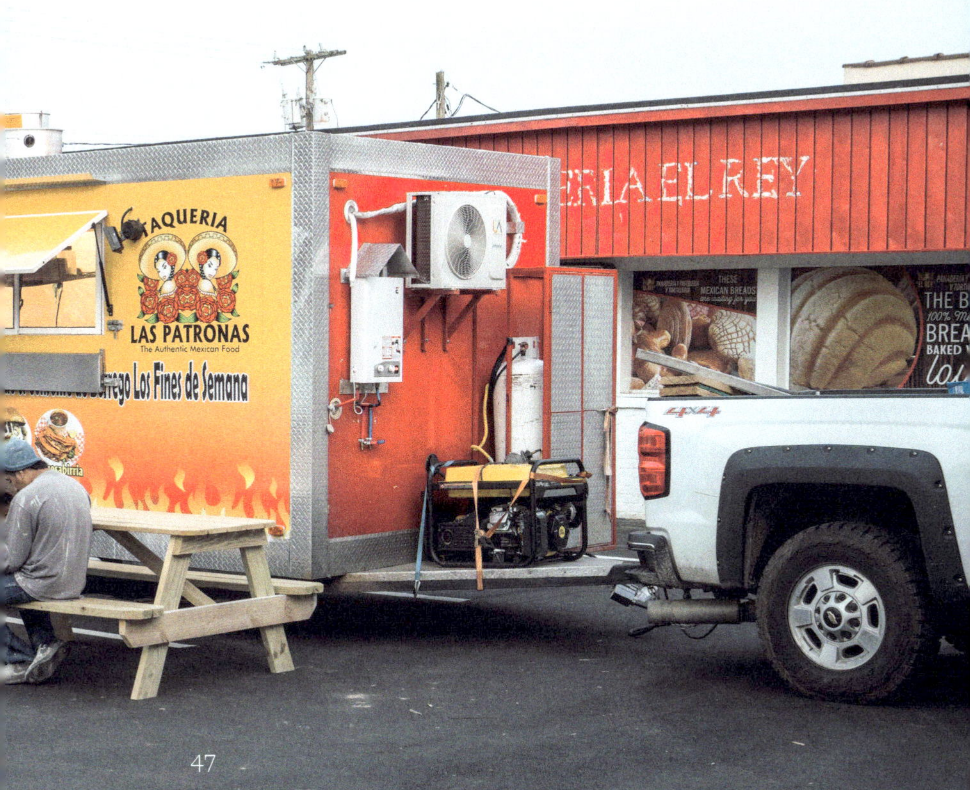
TAQUERIA
LAS PATRONAS
The Authentic Mexican Food
Los Fines de Semana
EL REY
THESE MEXICAN BREADS
4x4

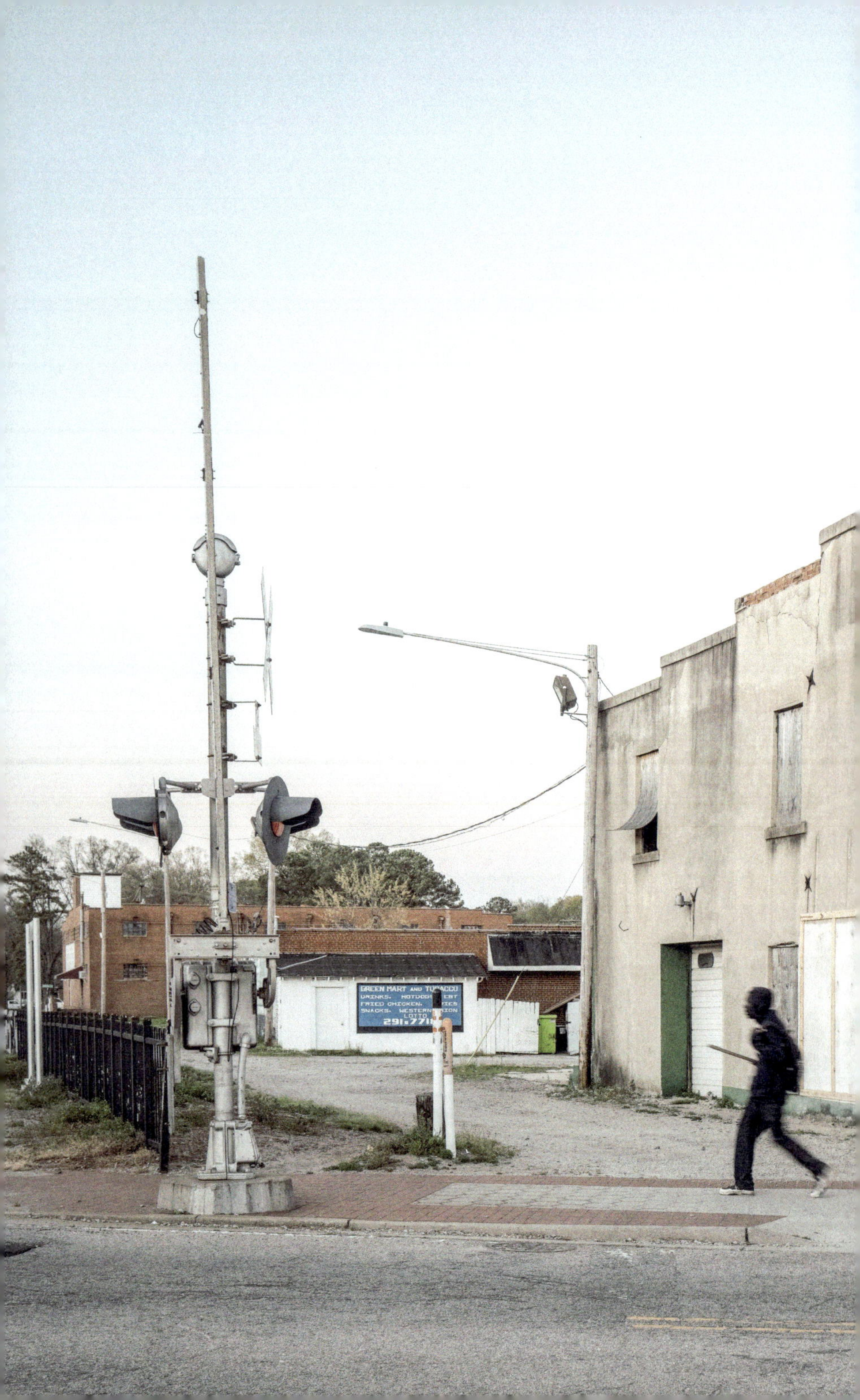
GREEN MART AND TO ACCO
DRINKS. HOTDOGS EBT
FRIED CHICKEN. ICS
SNACKS. WESTERN NION
LOTTO
291.771

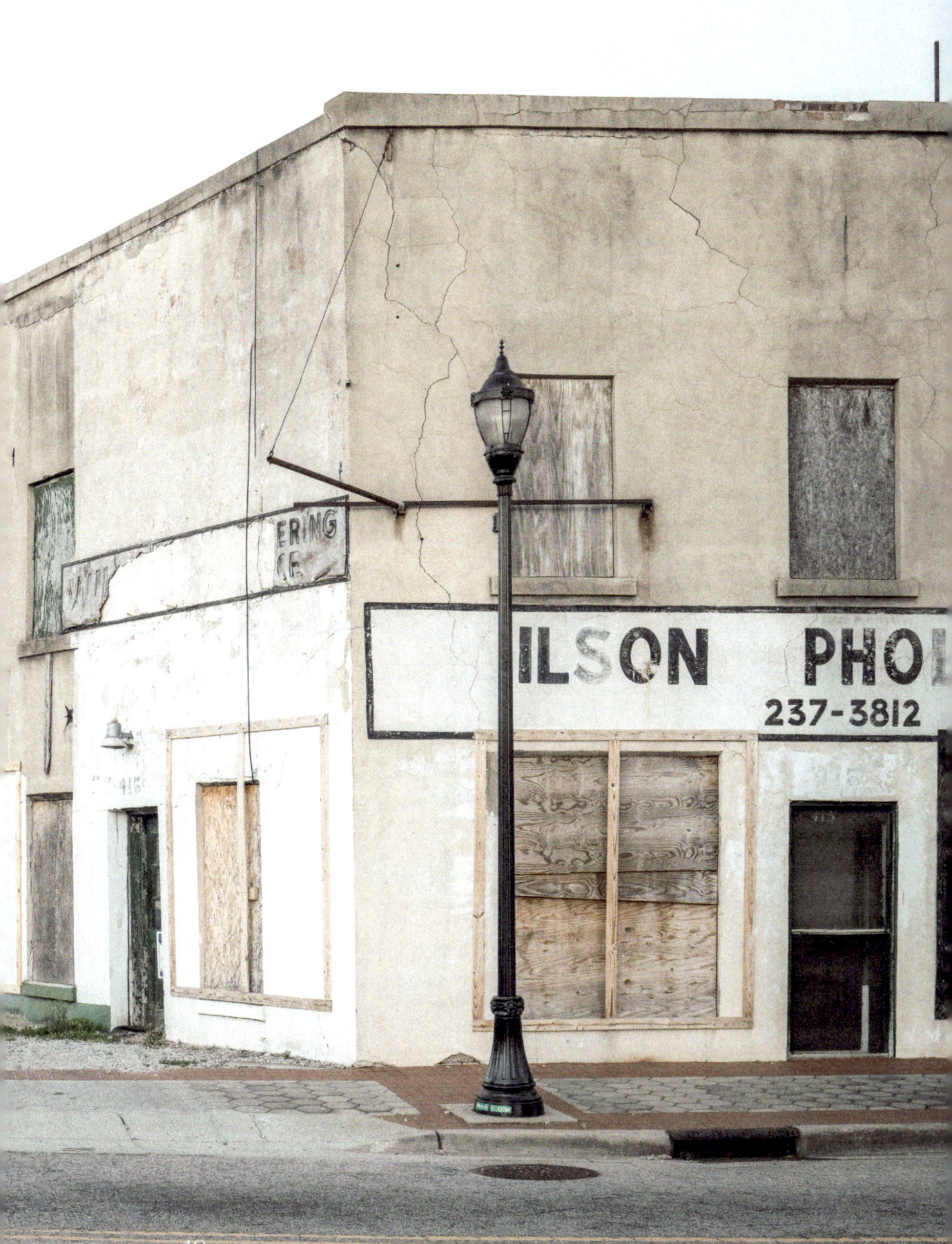
ERING
CE
ILSON PHO
237-3812

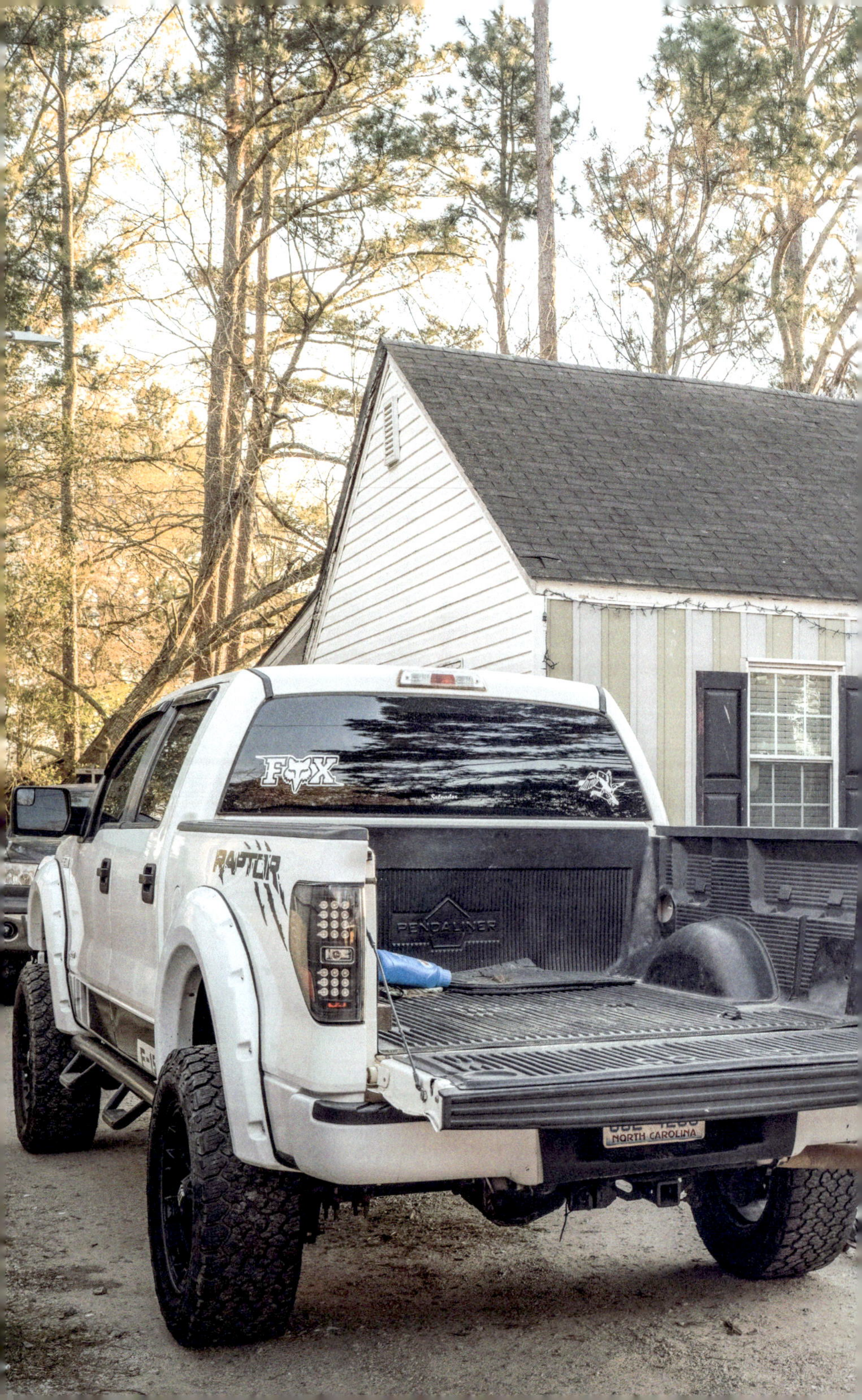
FOX
RAPTOR
PENDALINER
NORTH CAROLINA

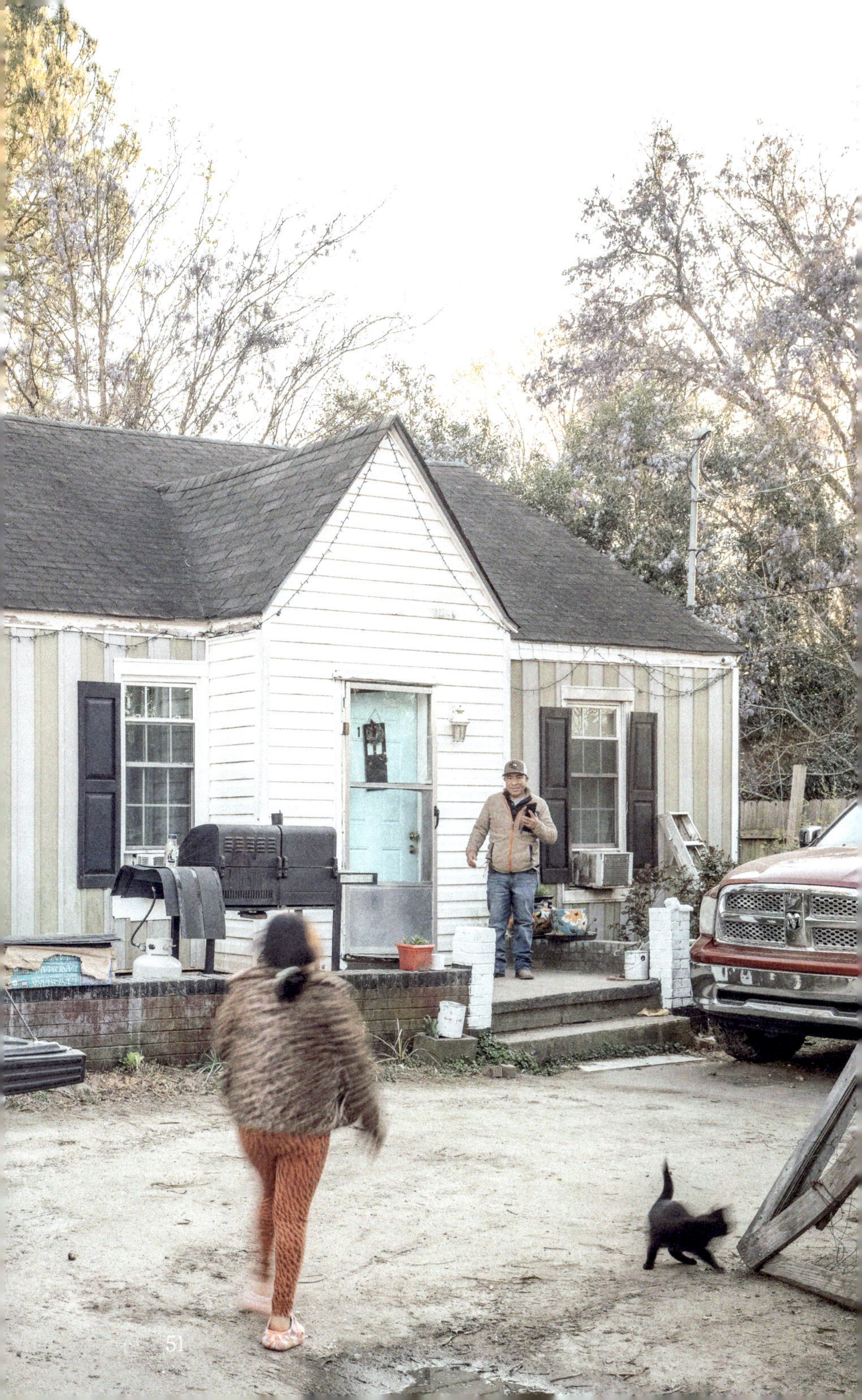

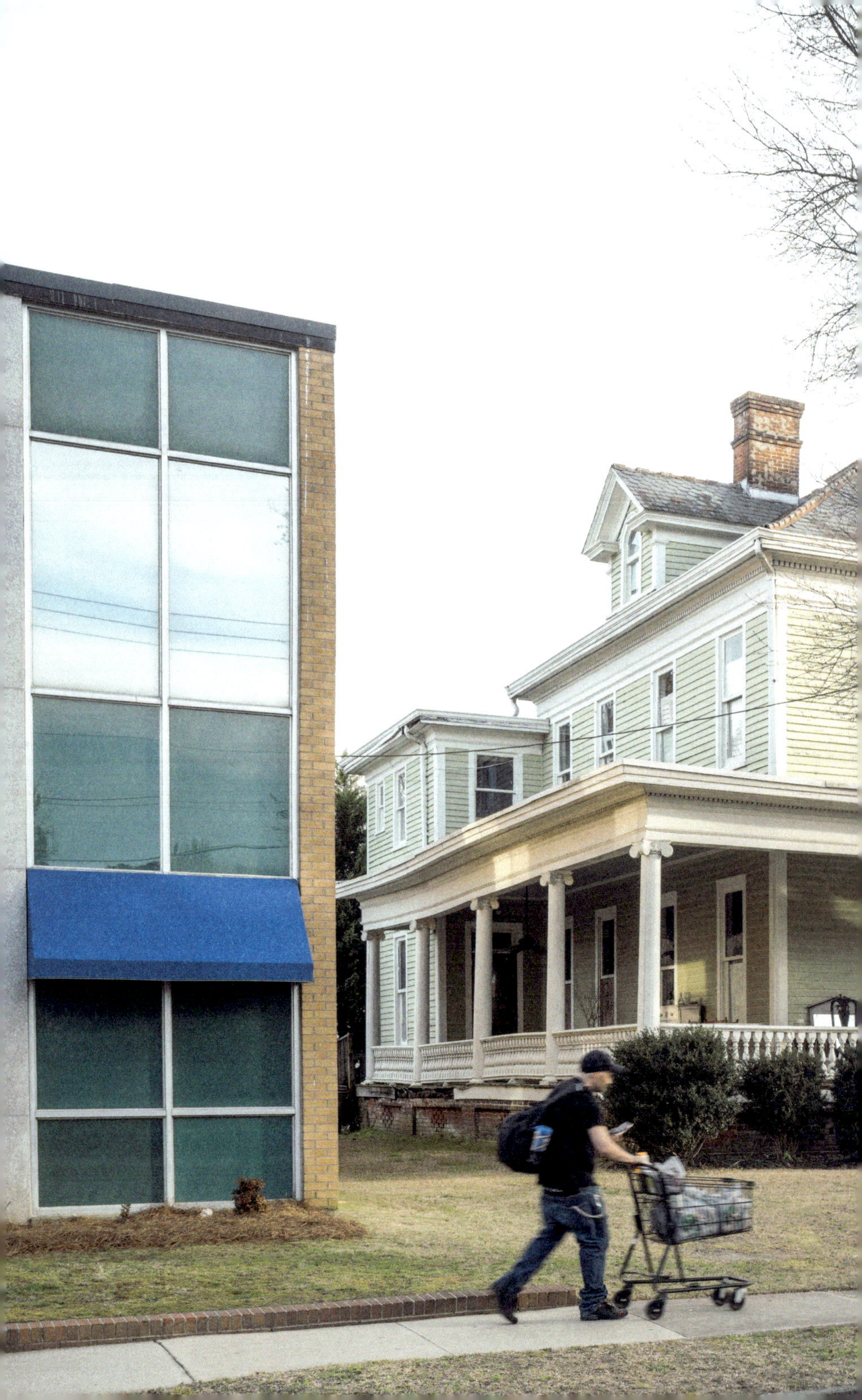

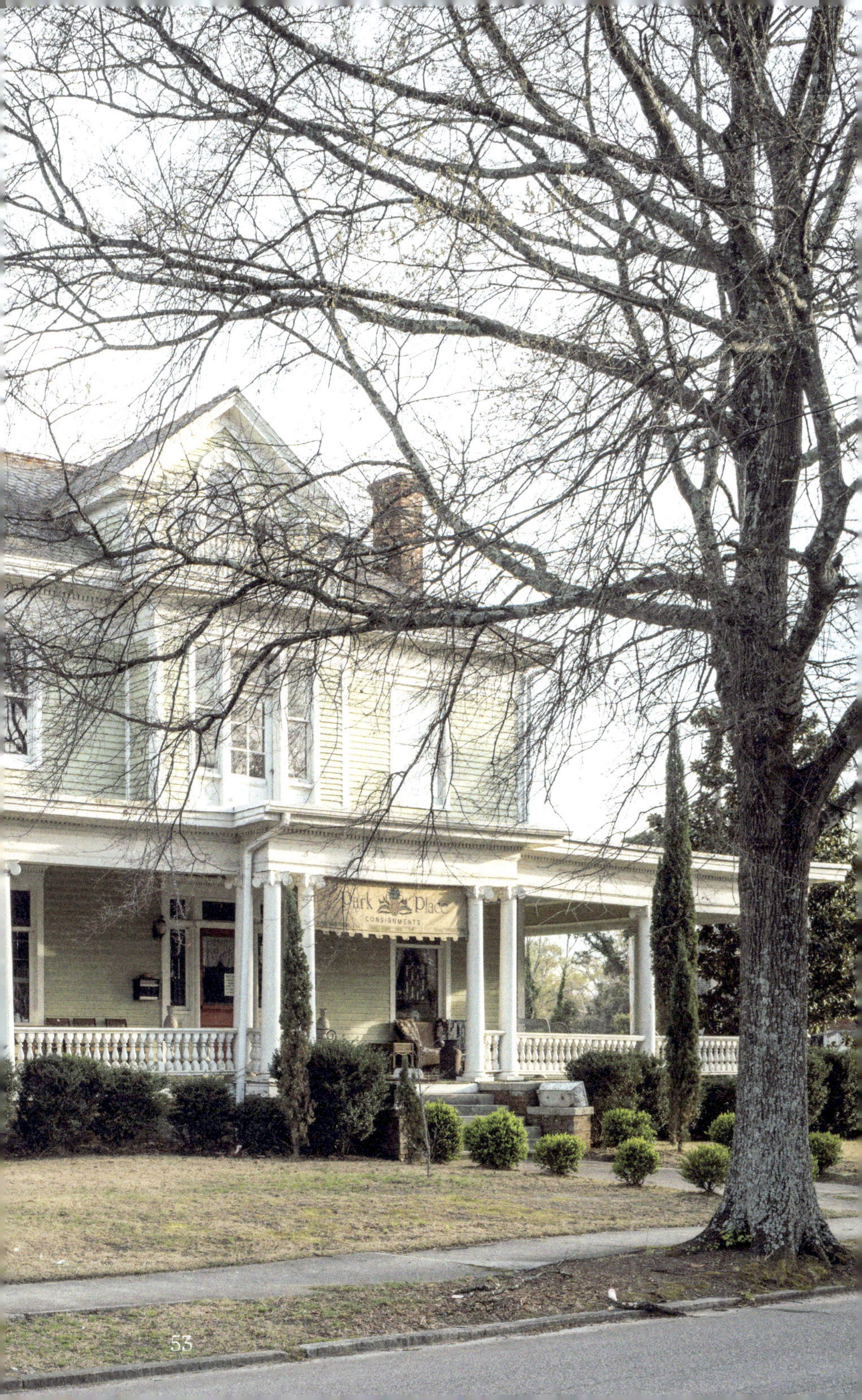
Park Place
CONSIGNMENTS

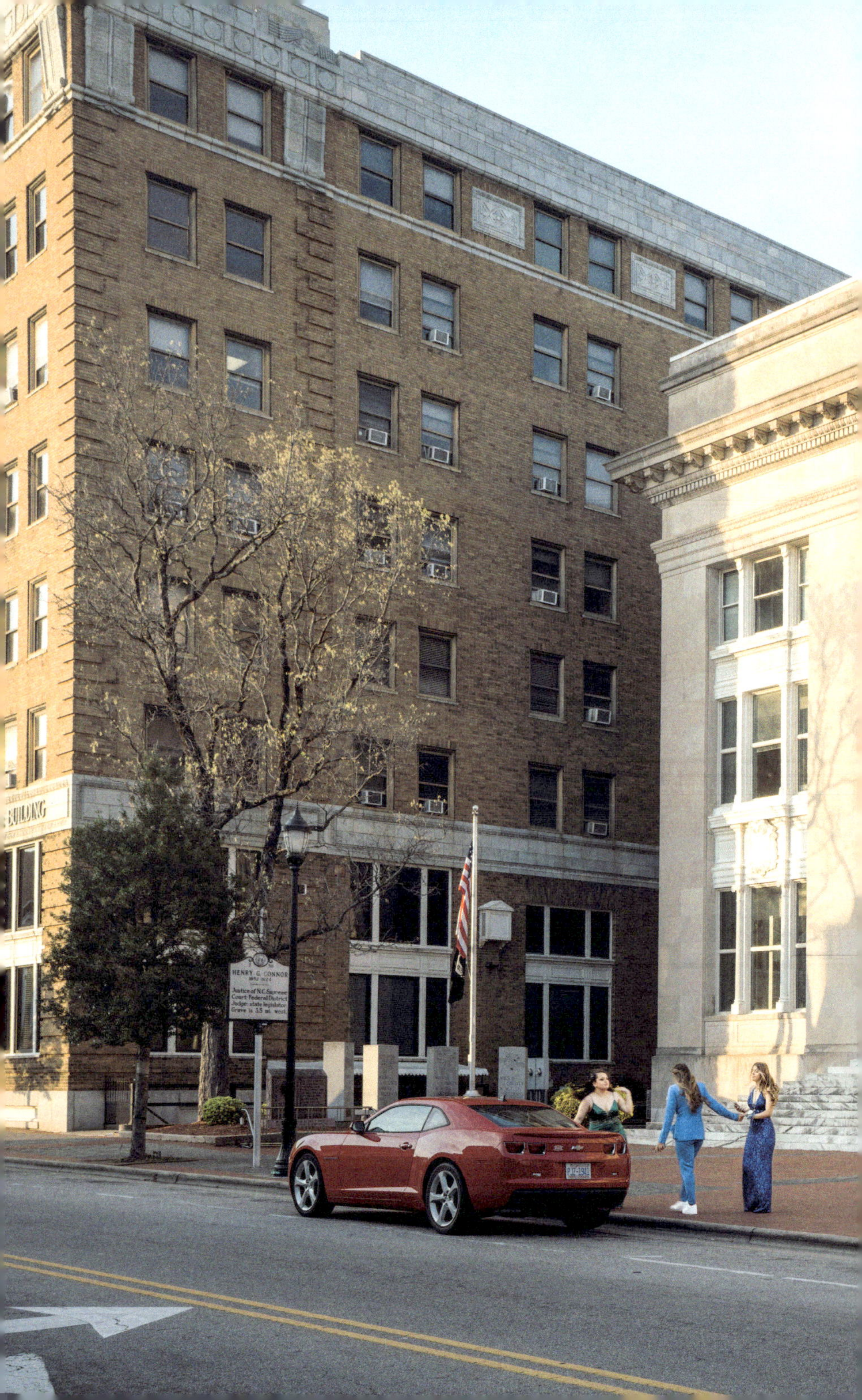
BUILDING
HENRY G. CONNOR
Justice of N.C. Supreme Court; Federal District Judge; state legislator. Grave is 3.5 mi. west.

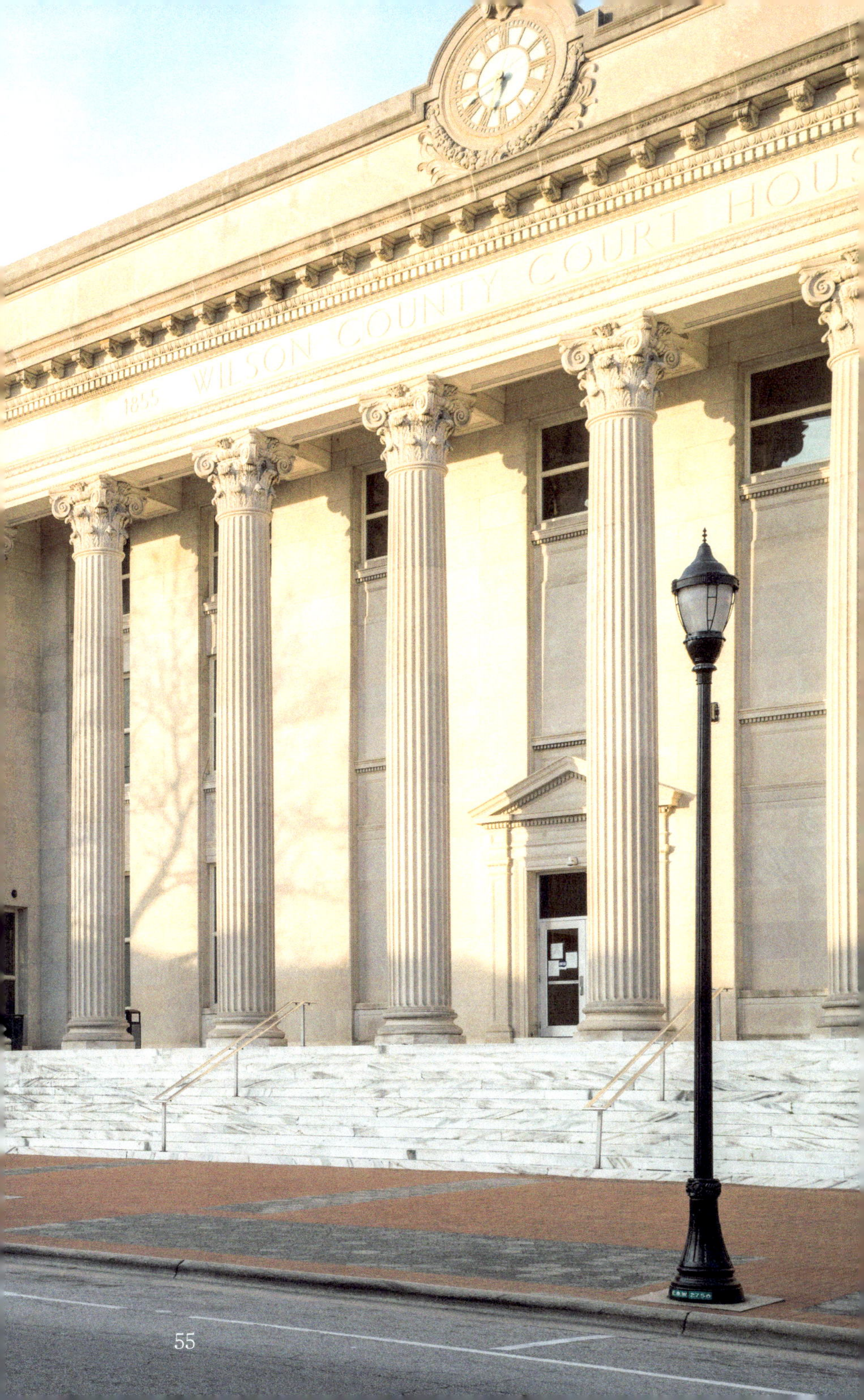
1855 WILSON COUNTY COURT HOUS

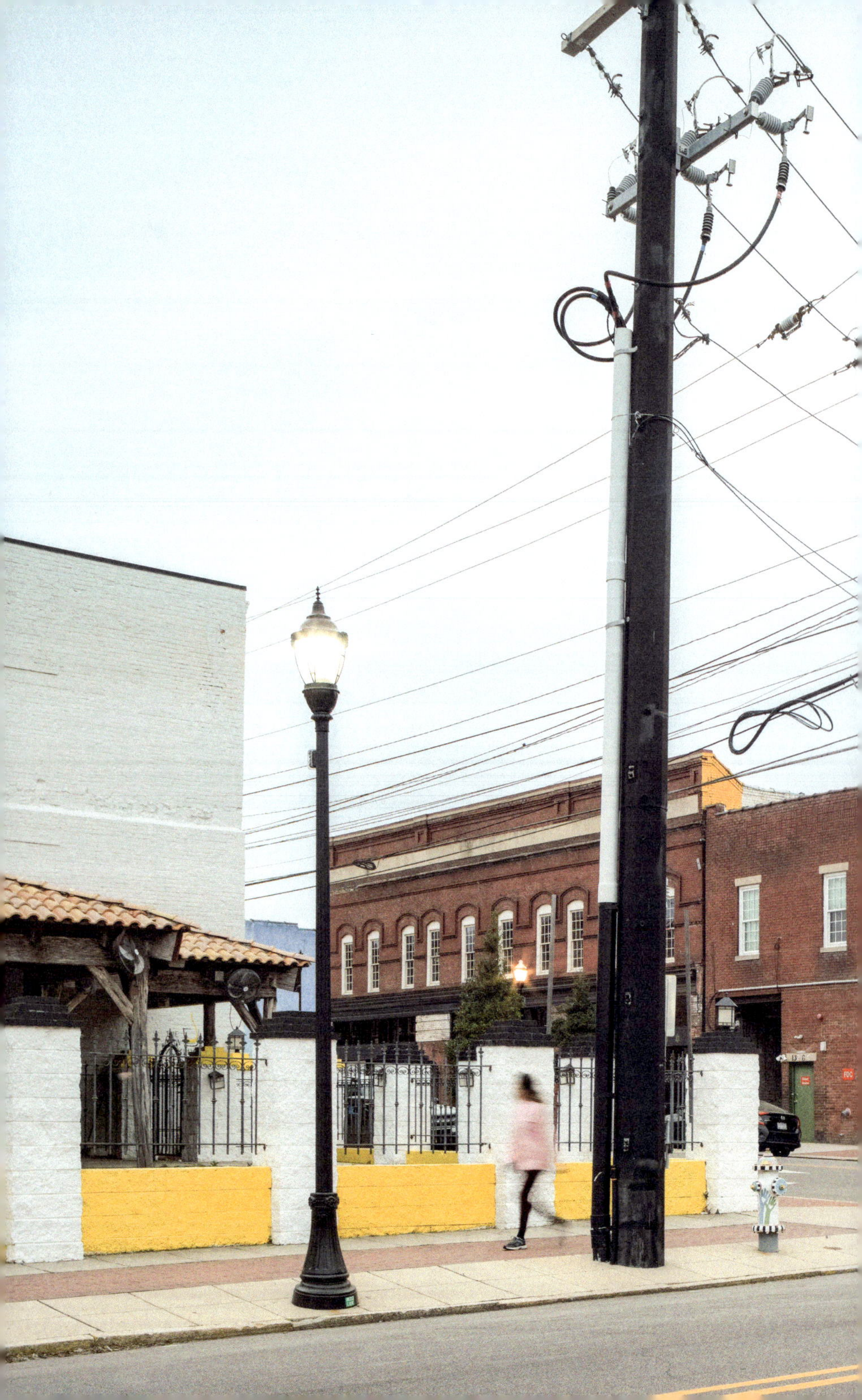

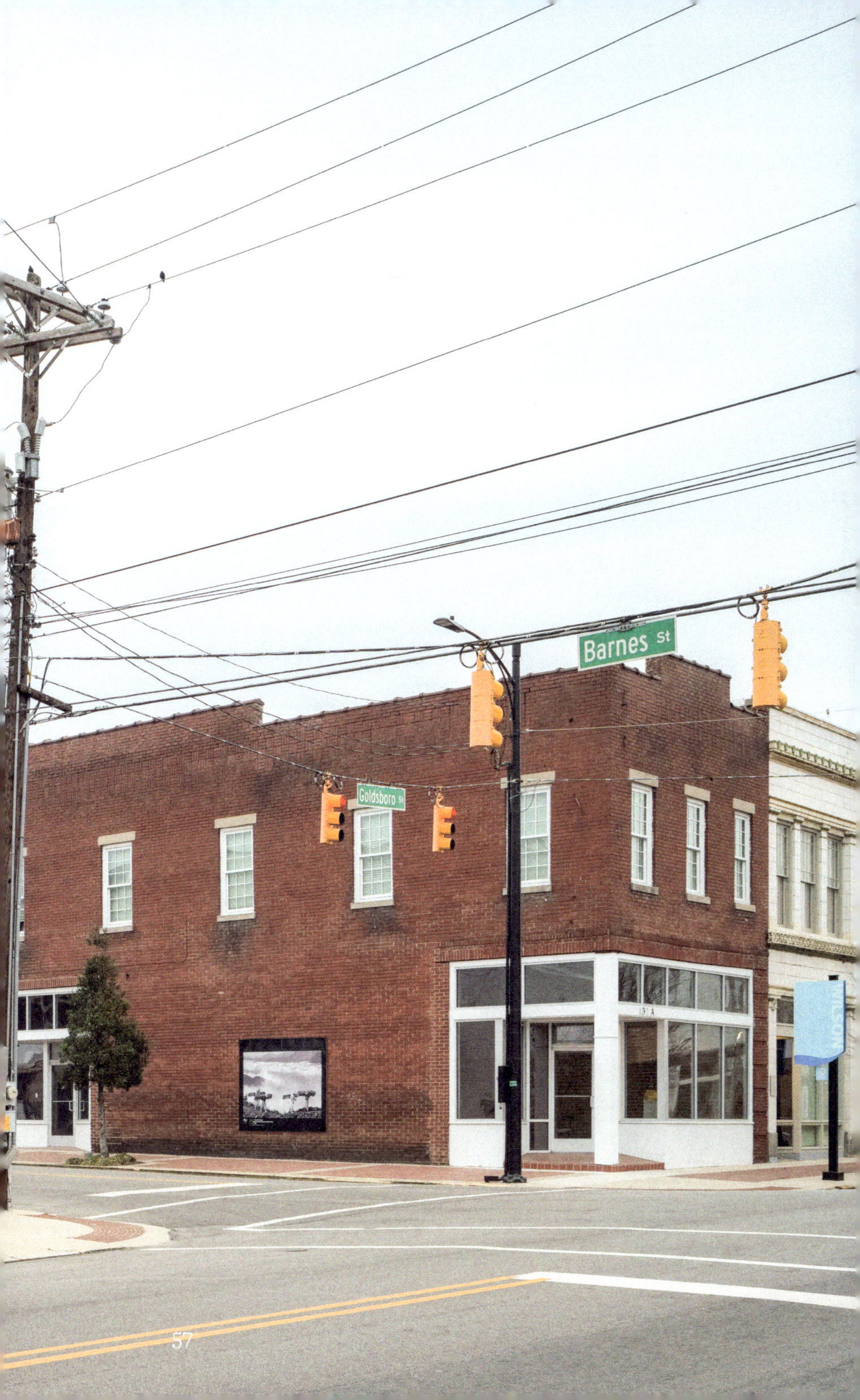
Barnes St
Goldsboro St

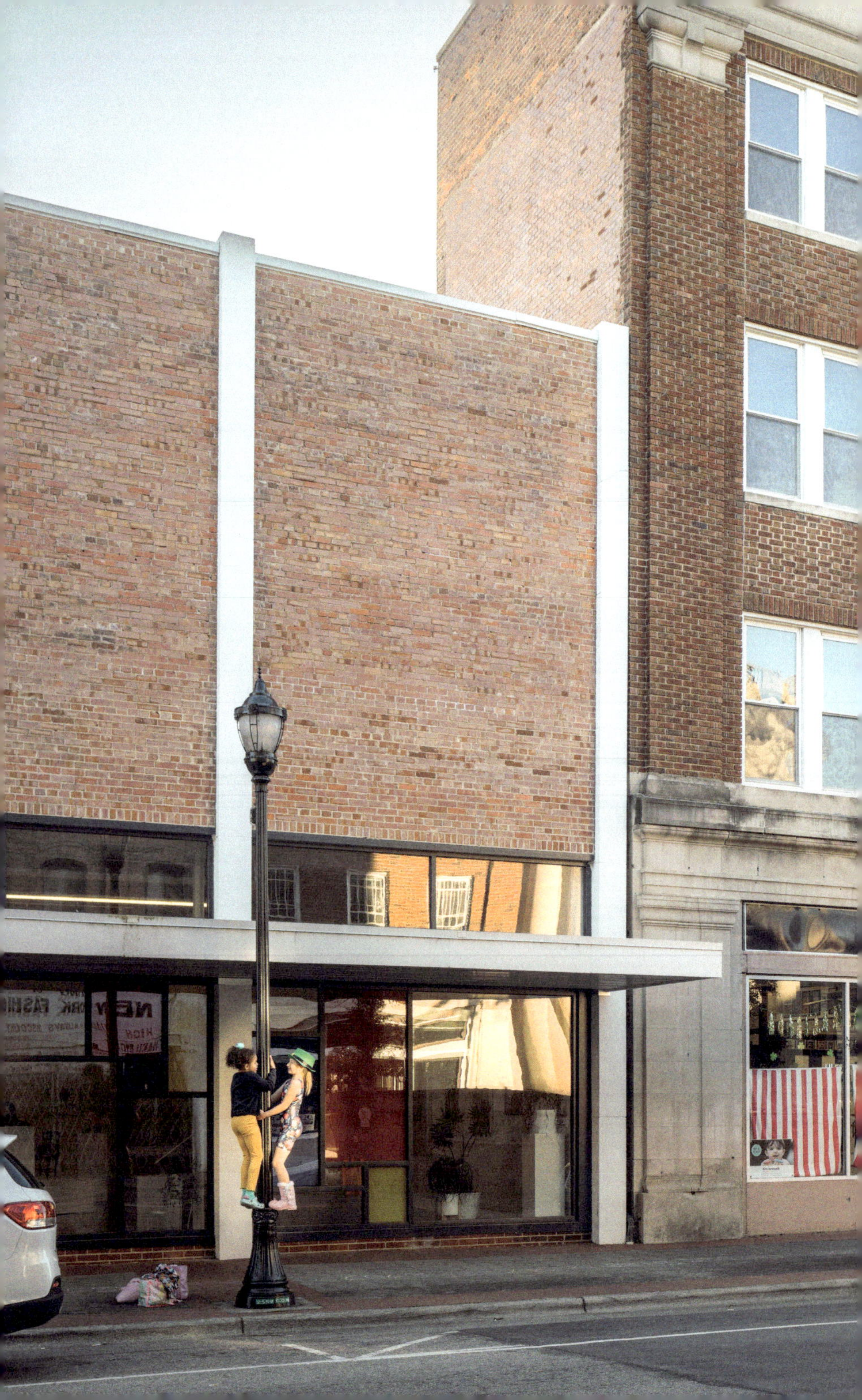

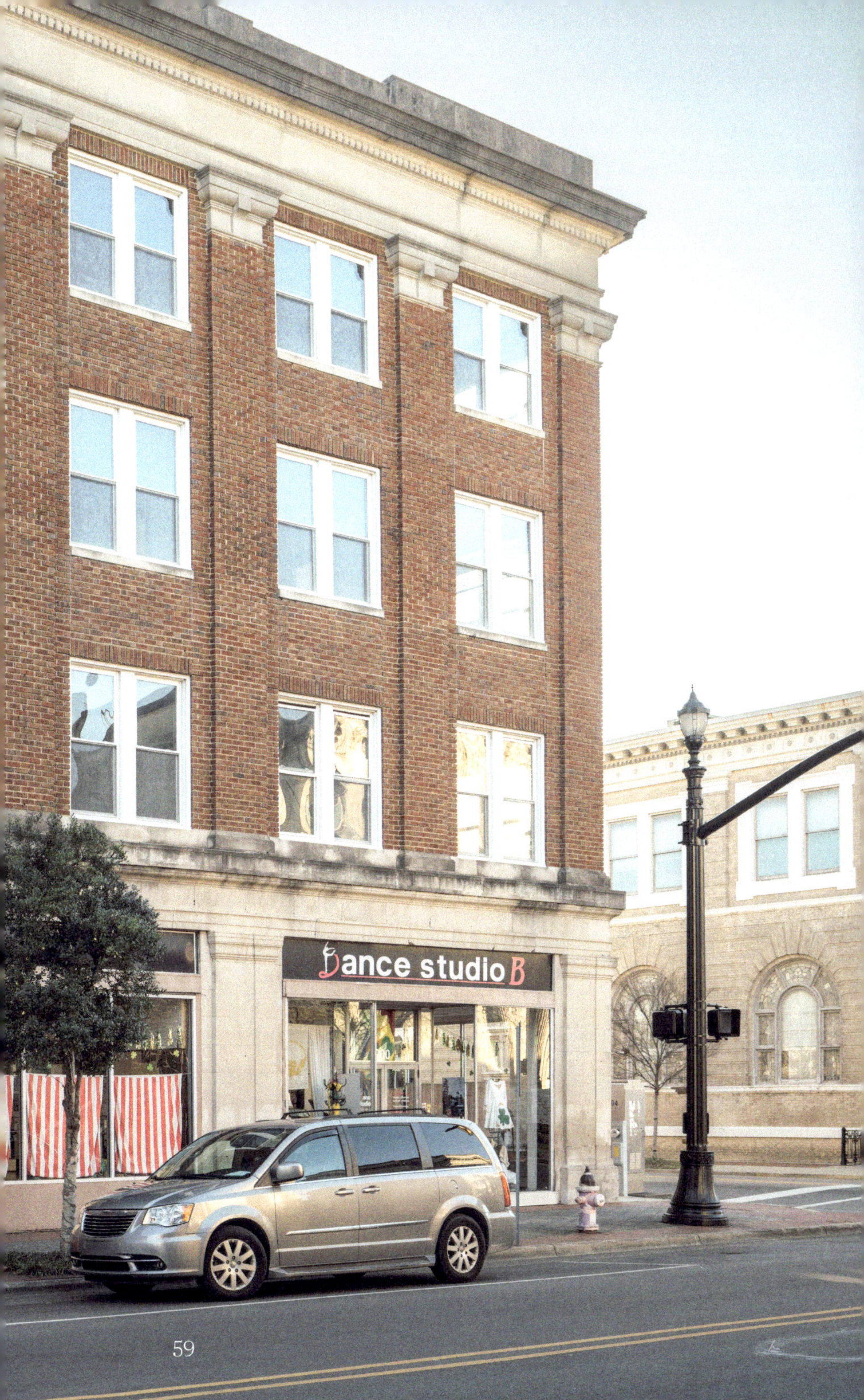
Dance studio B

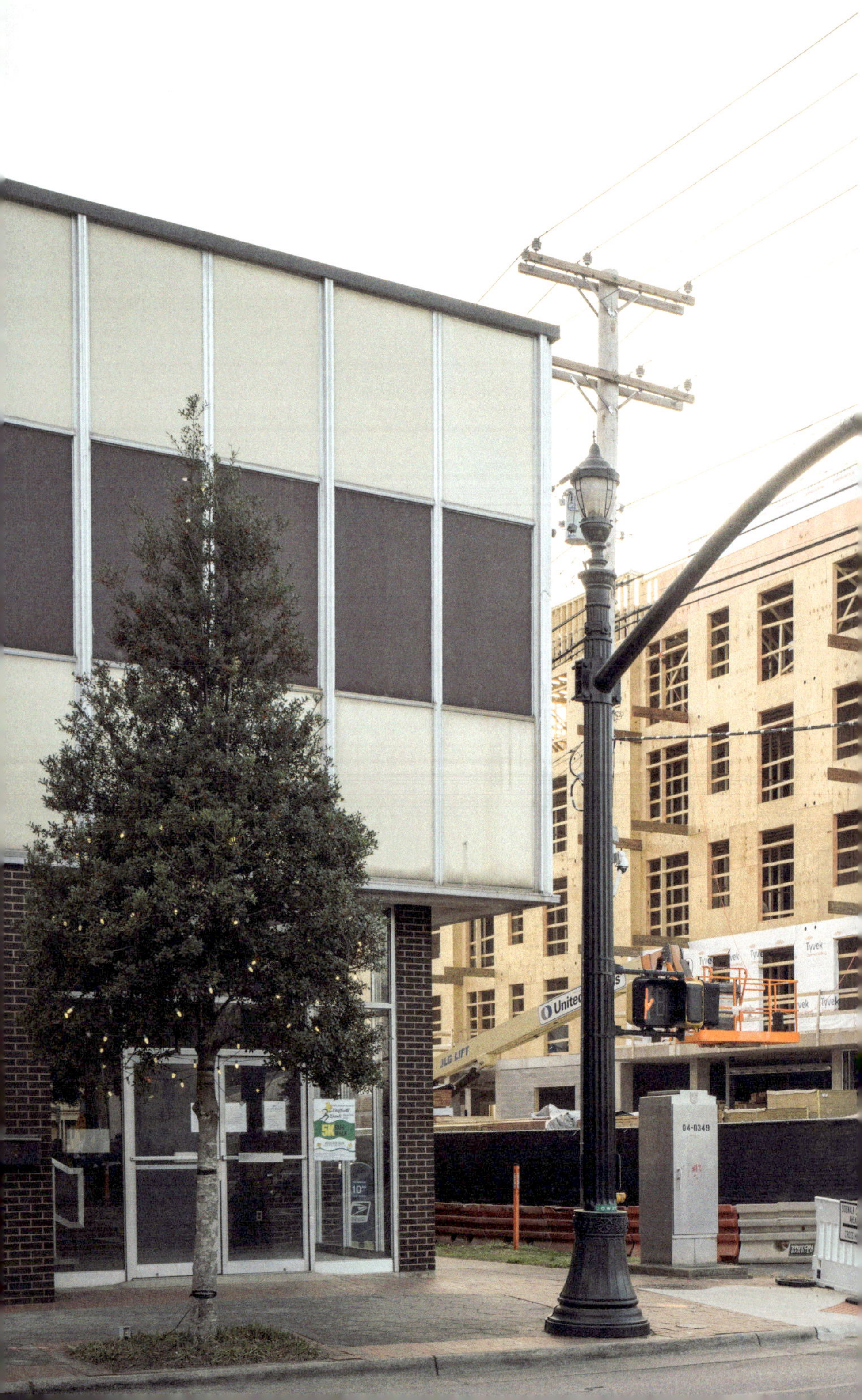
5K
JLG LIFT
Tyvek
04-0349

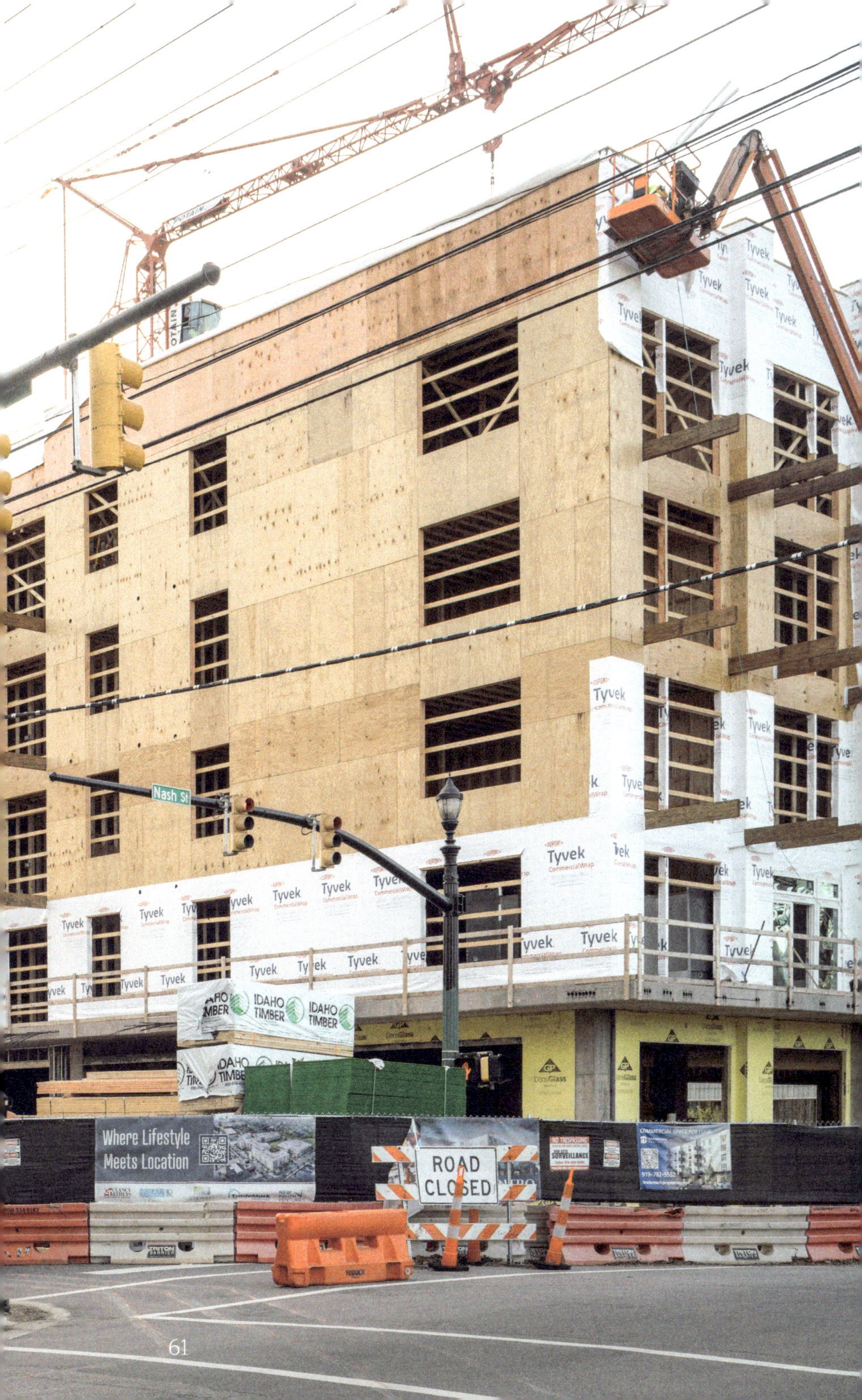
Tyvek
IDAHO TIMBER
Nash St
Where Lifestyle
Meets Location
ROAD
CLOSED

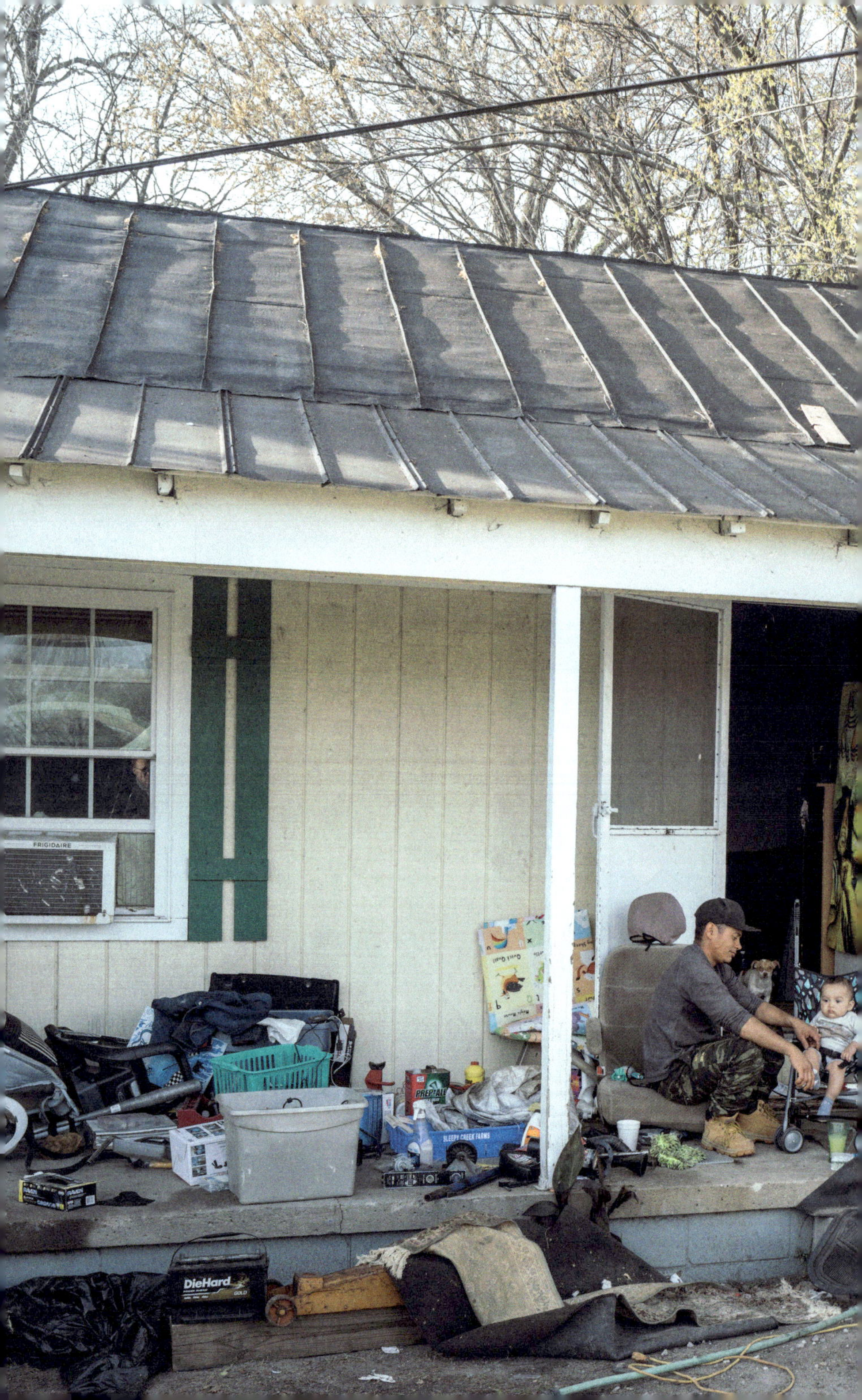
FRIGIDAIRE
PREP-ALL
SLEEPY CREEK FARMS
DieHard
GOLD

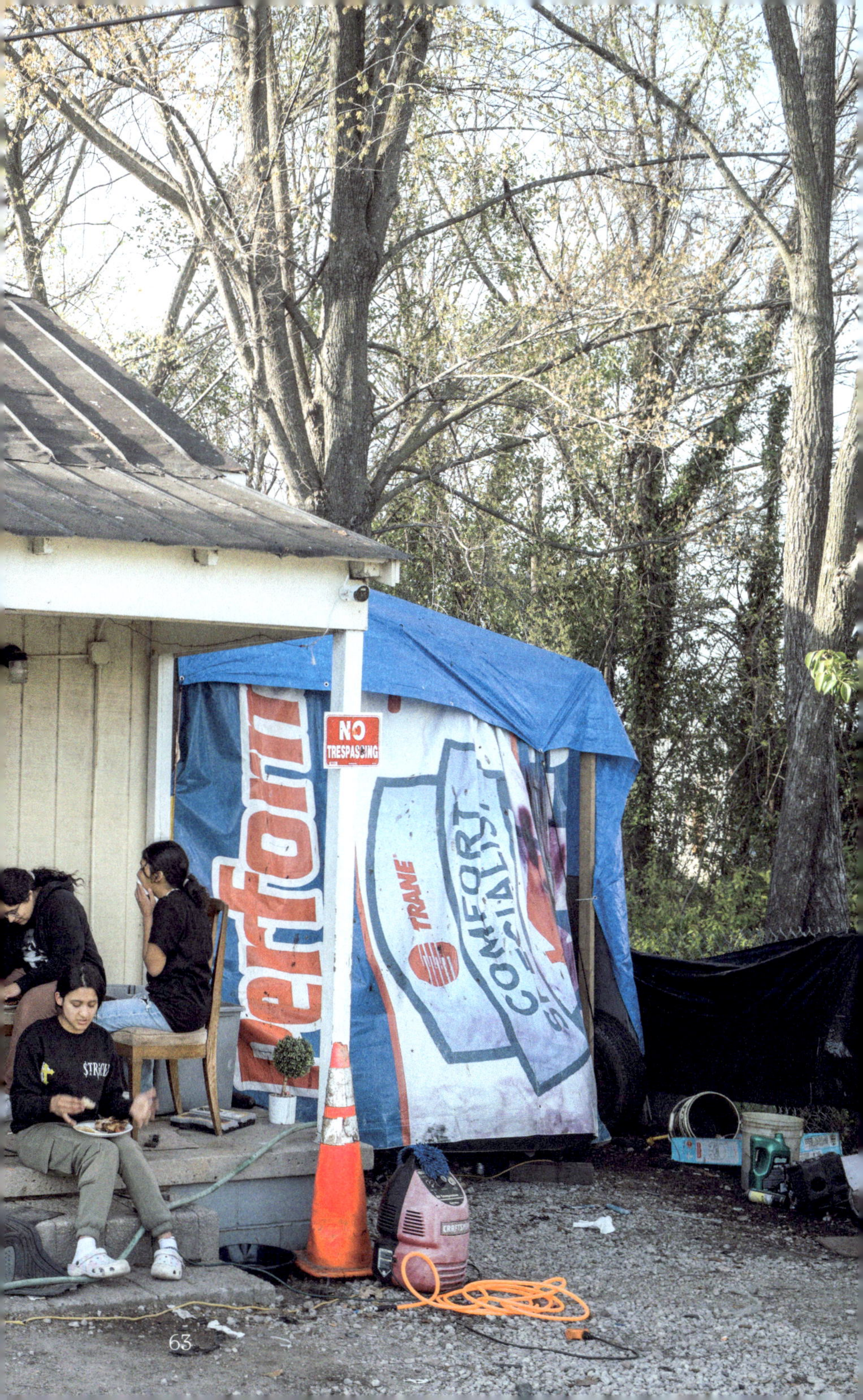
NO
TRESPASSING
TRANE
COMFORT

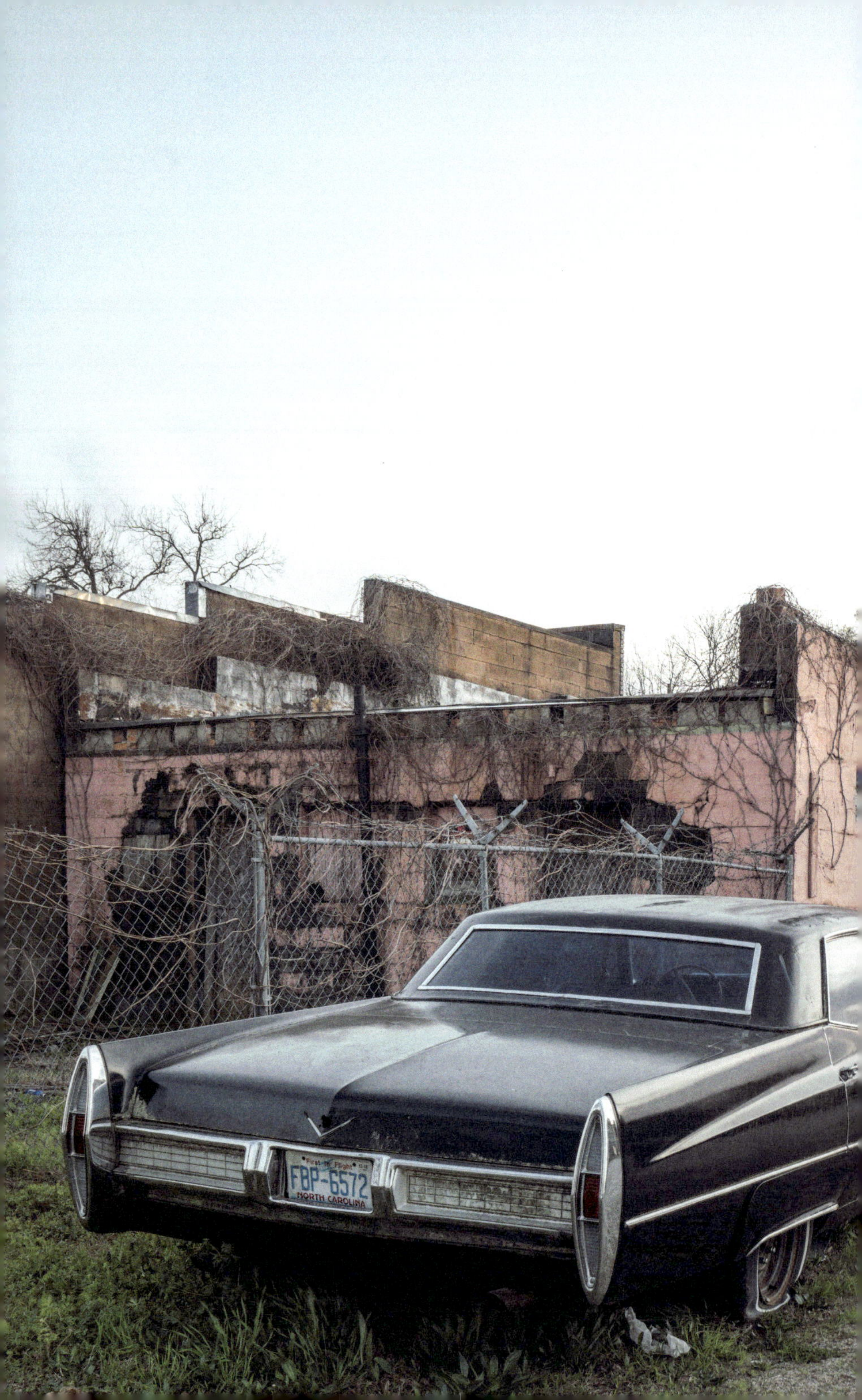
First in Flight
FBP-6572
NORTH CAROLINA

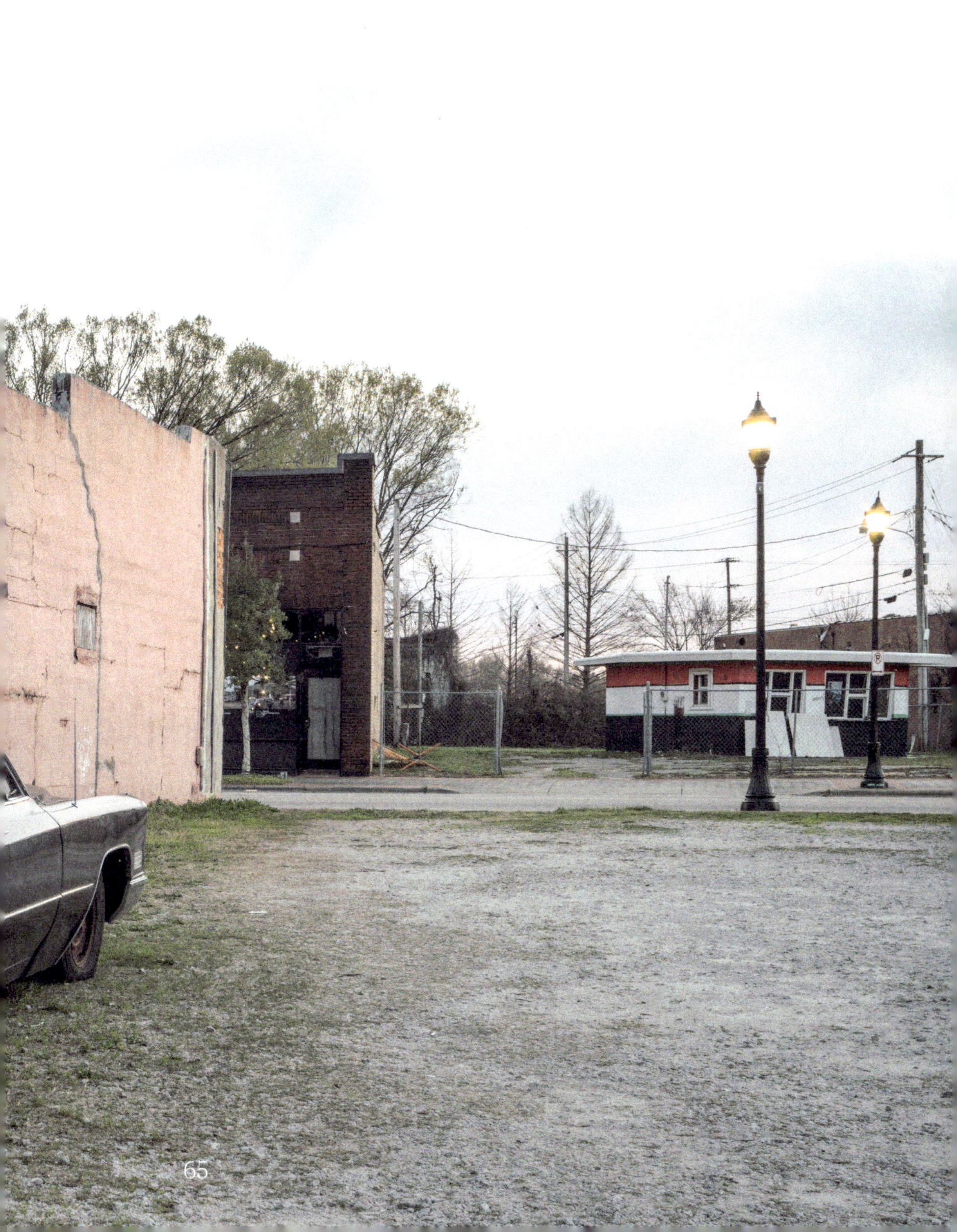

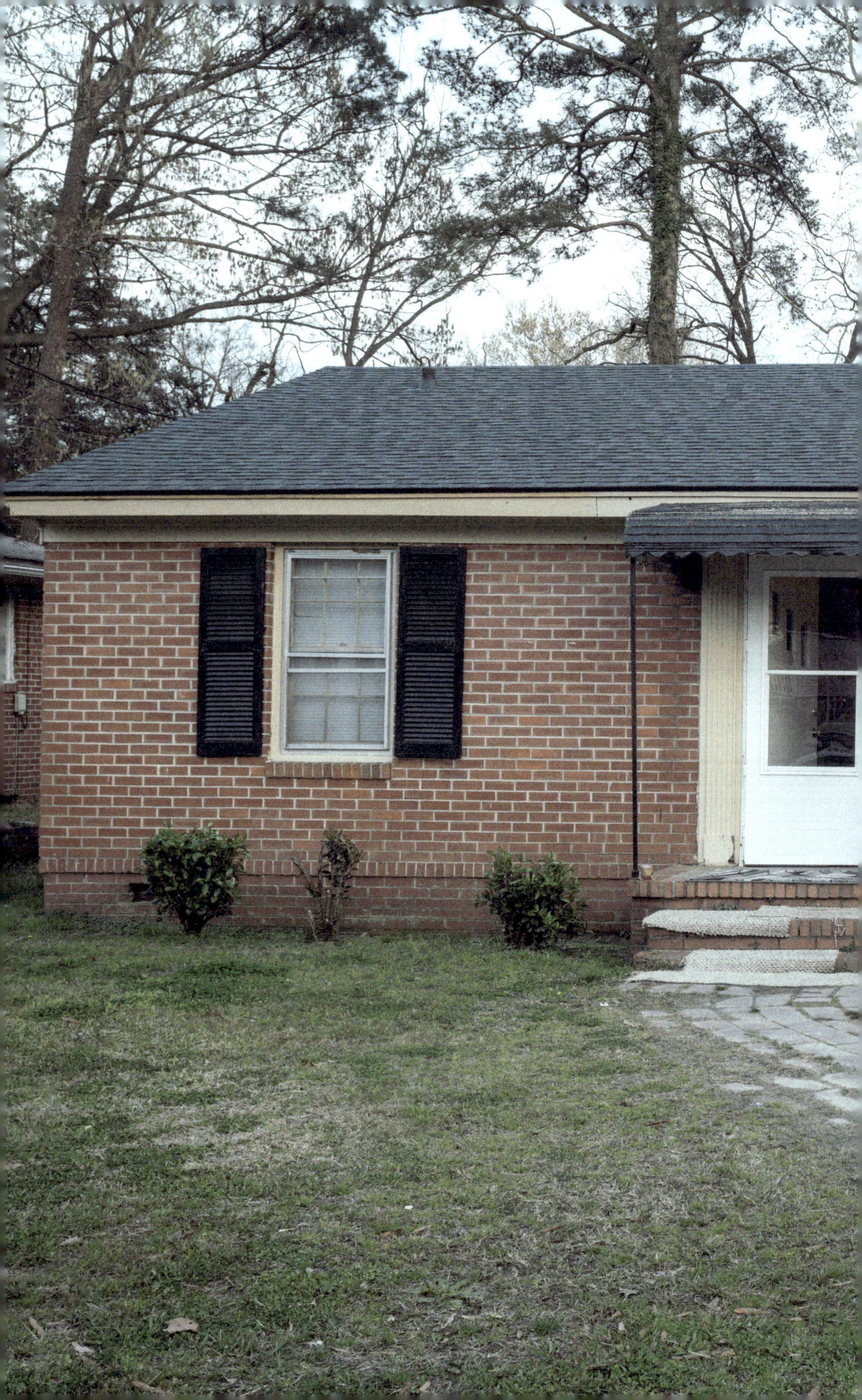

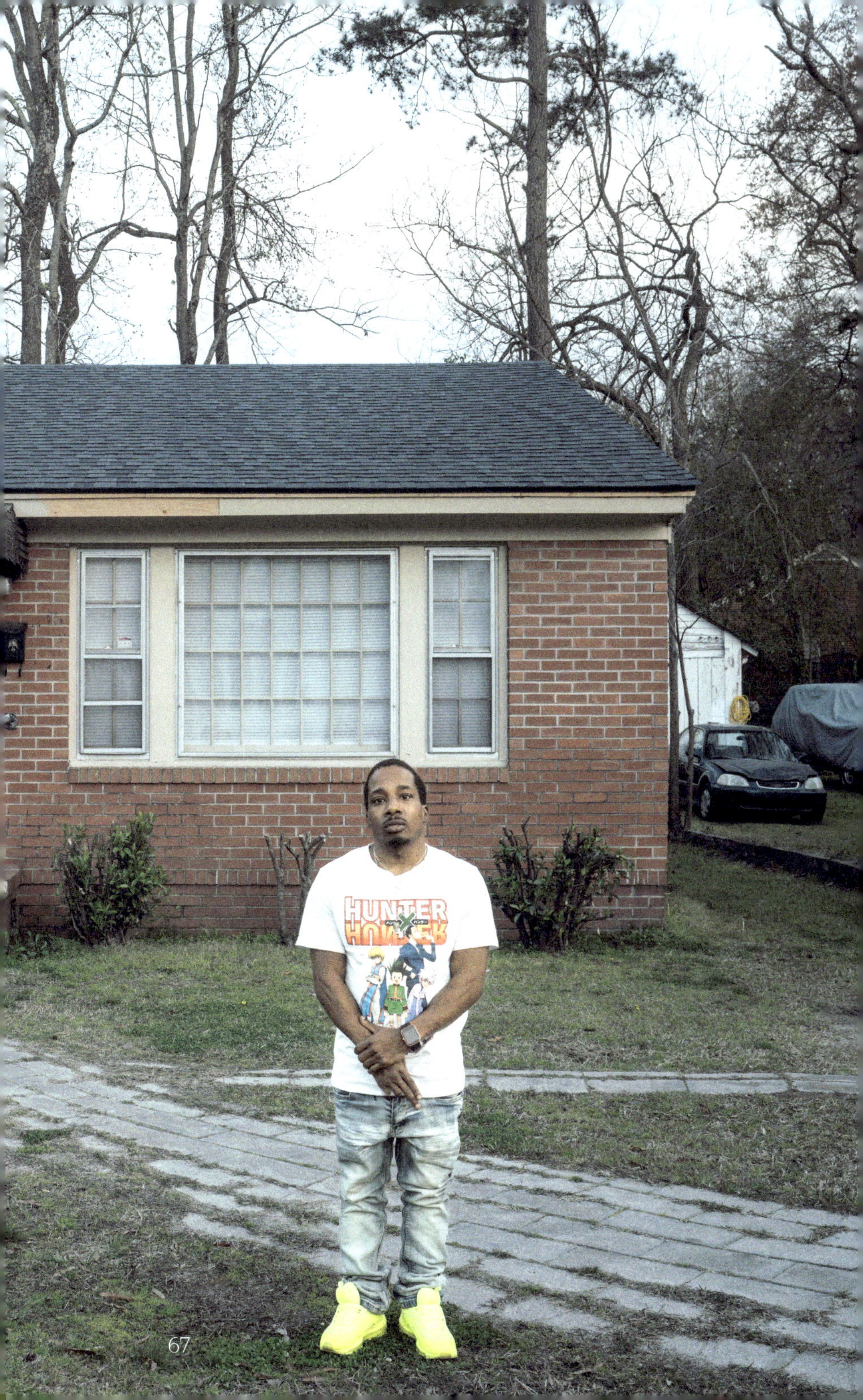
HUNTER

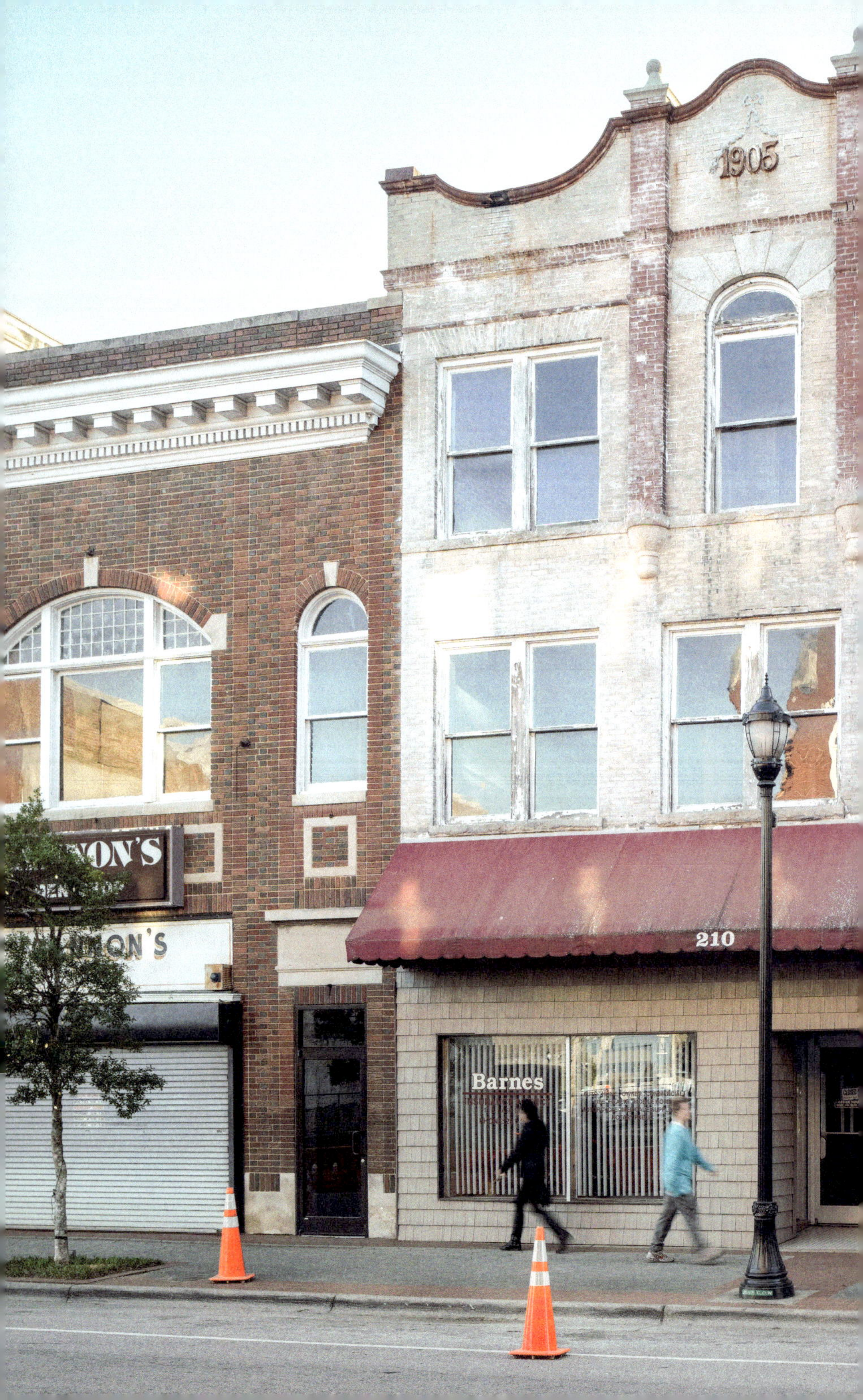
1905
210
Barnes

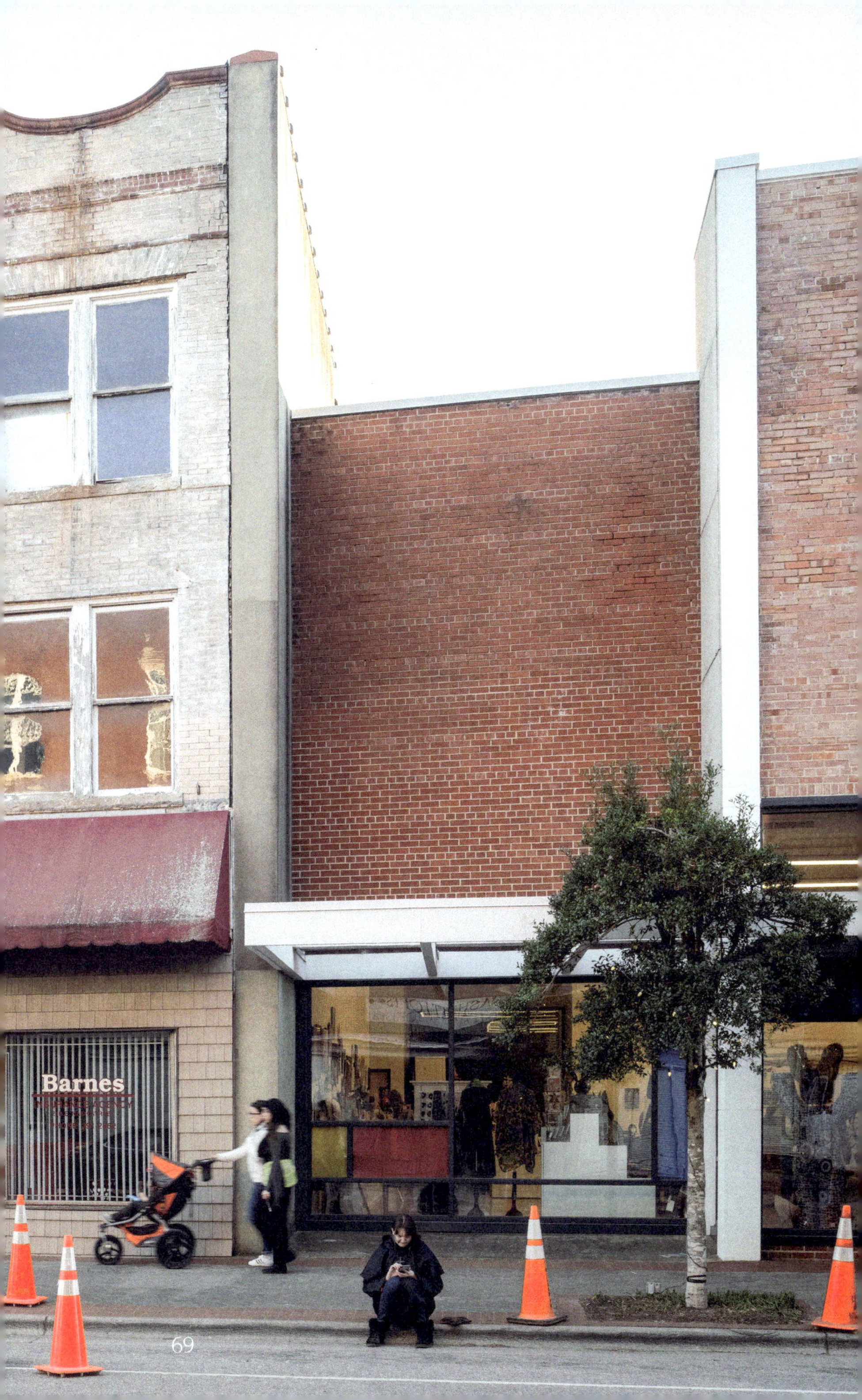
Barnes

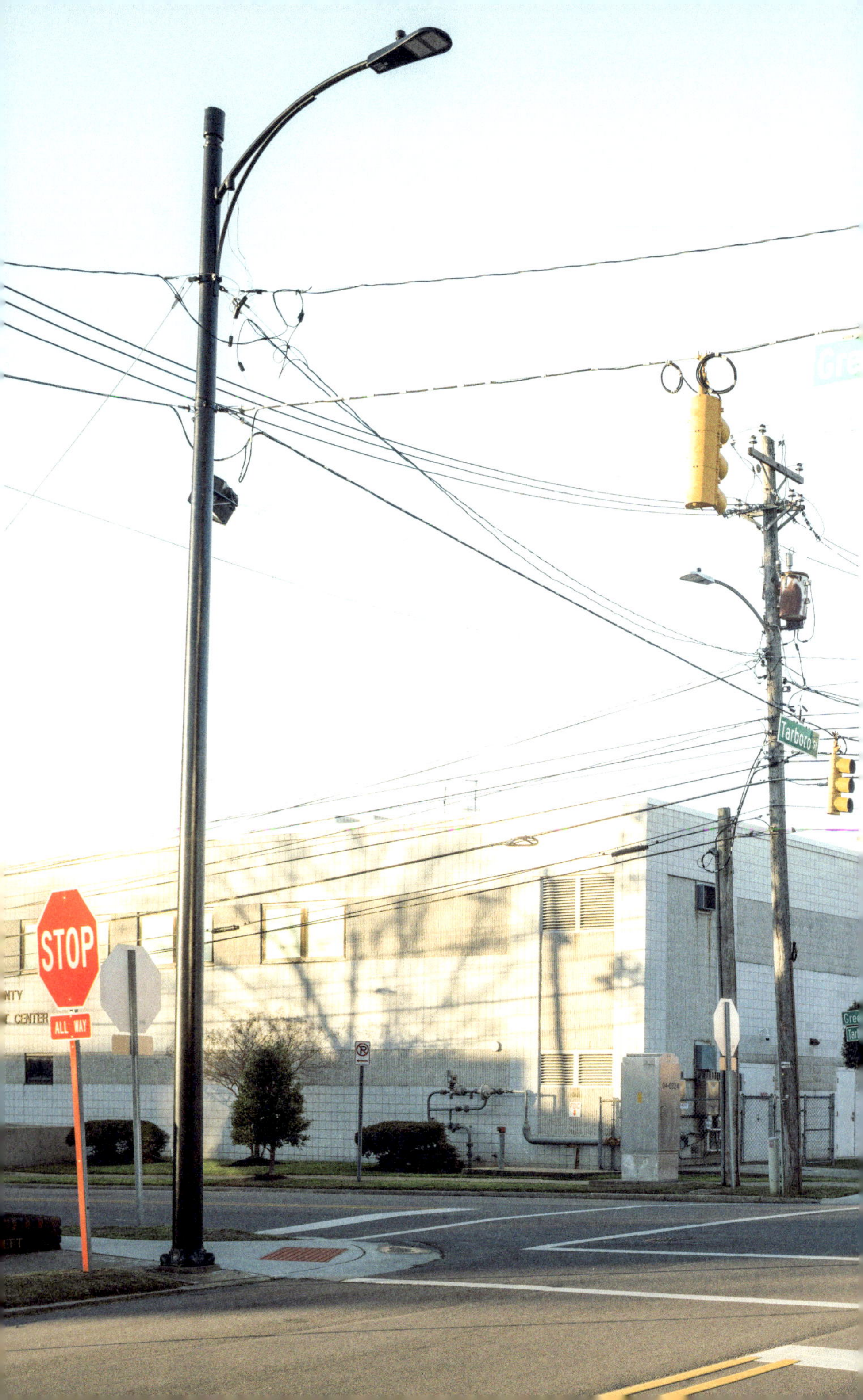

STOP
ALL WAY
Tarboro

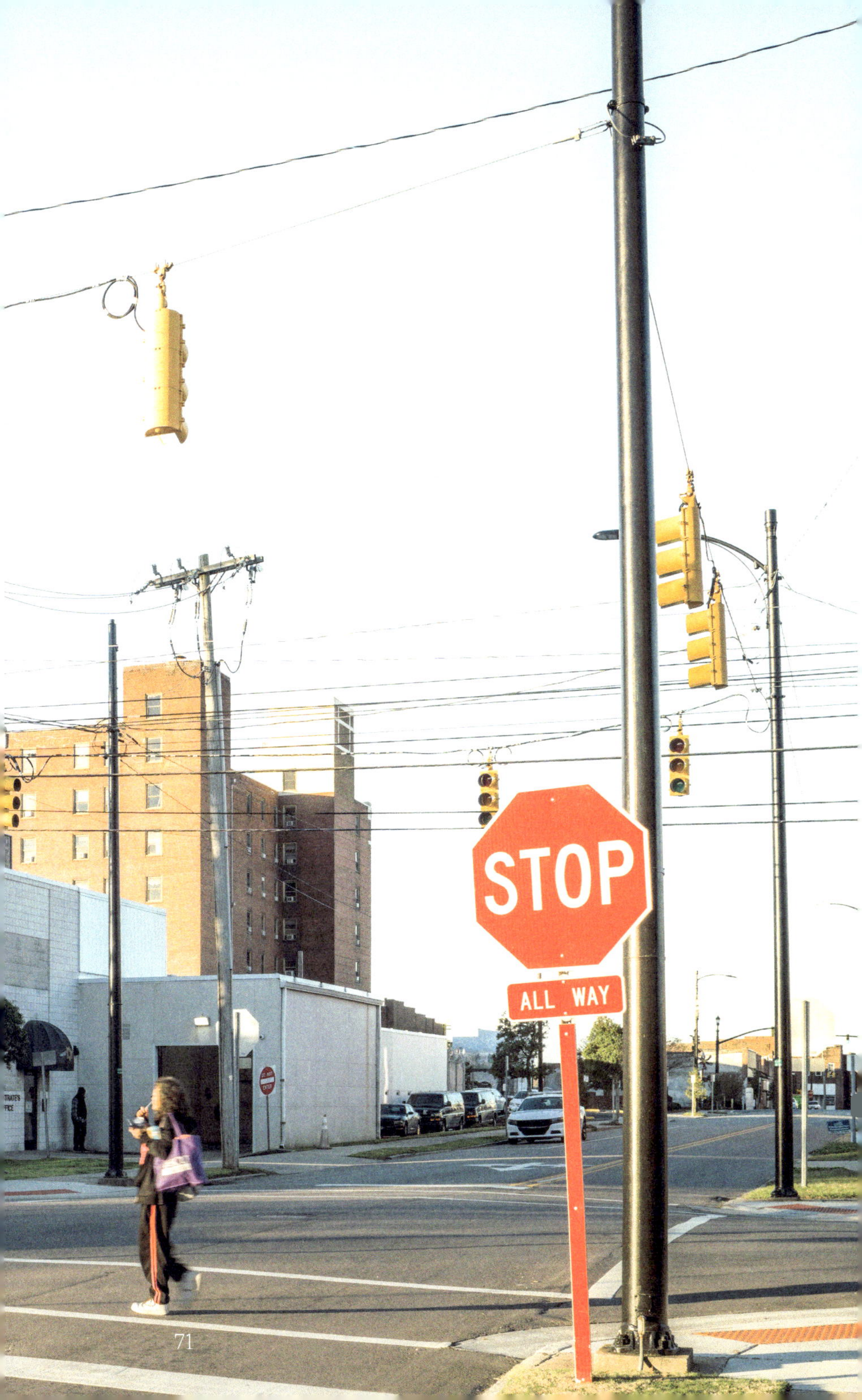
STOP
ALL WAY

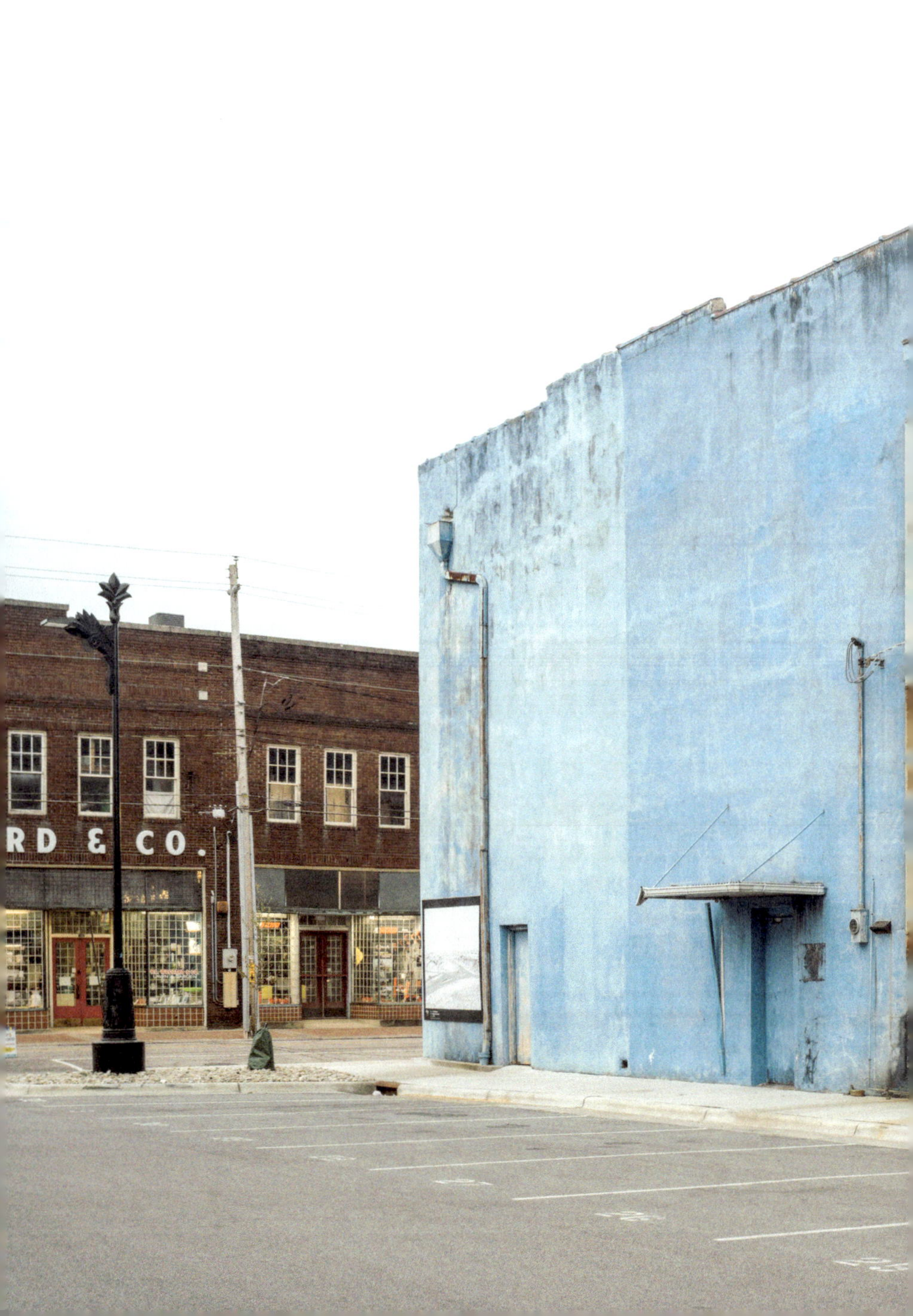
RD & CO.

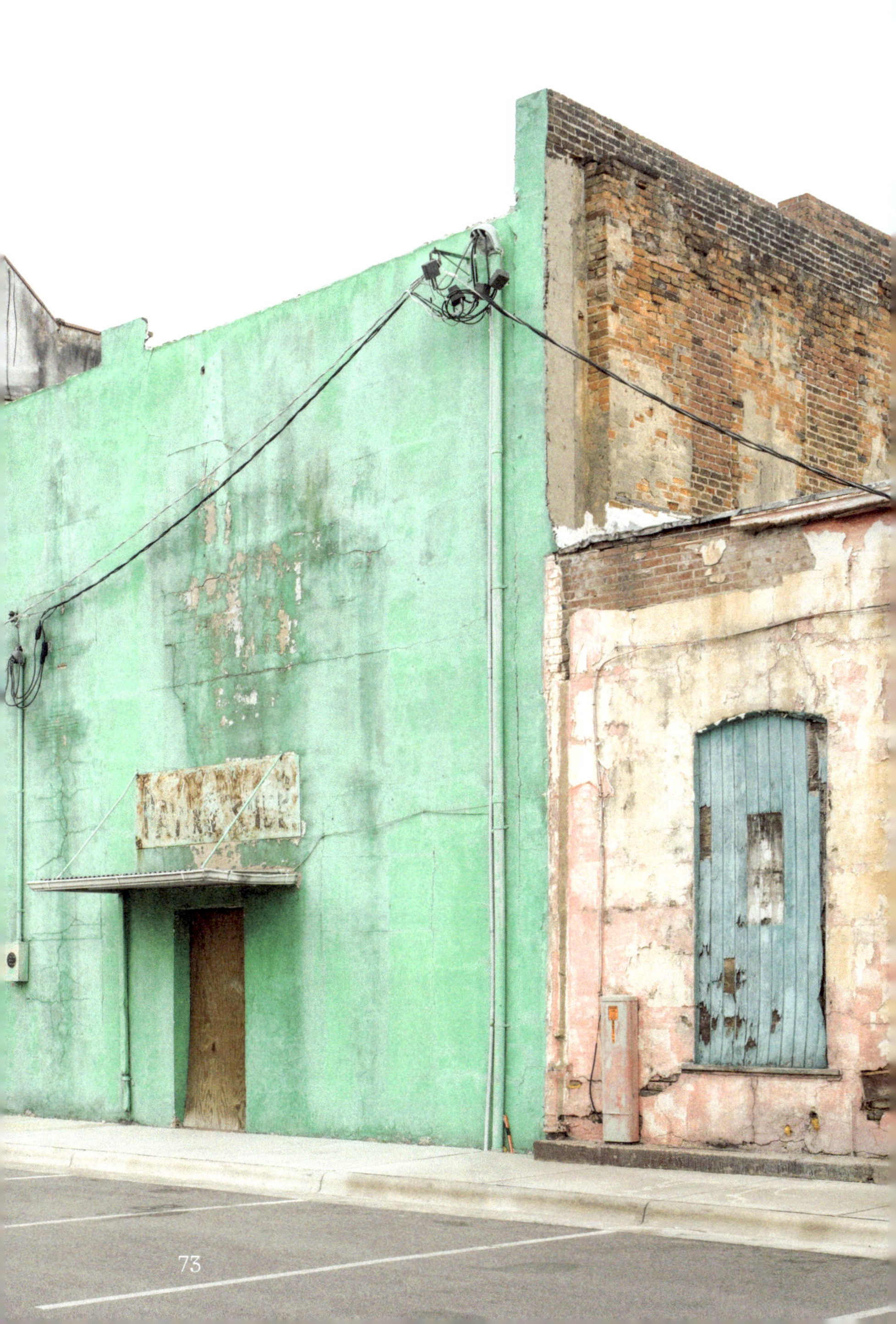

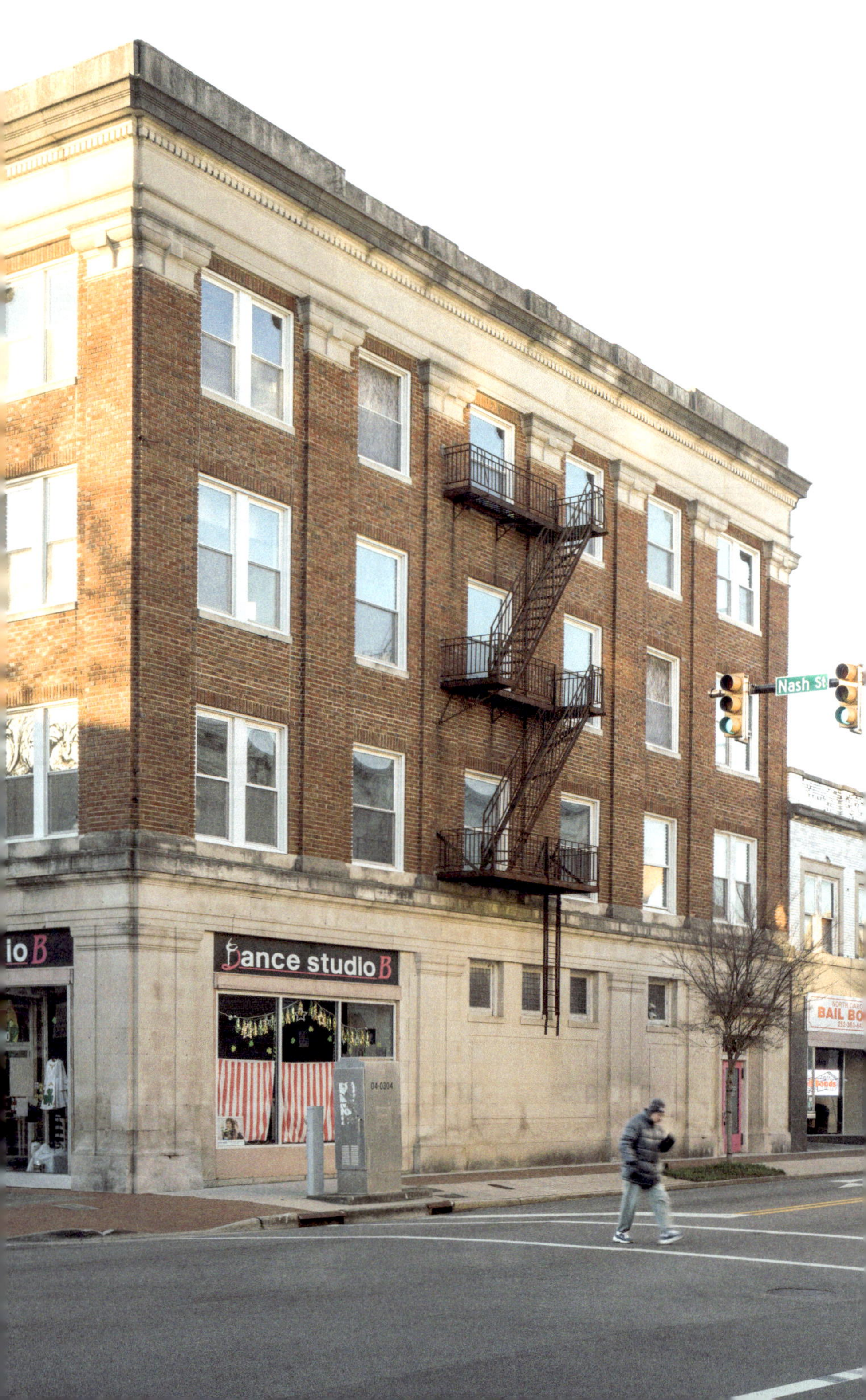
Dance studio B
Nash St
BAIL BO

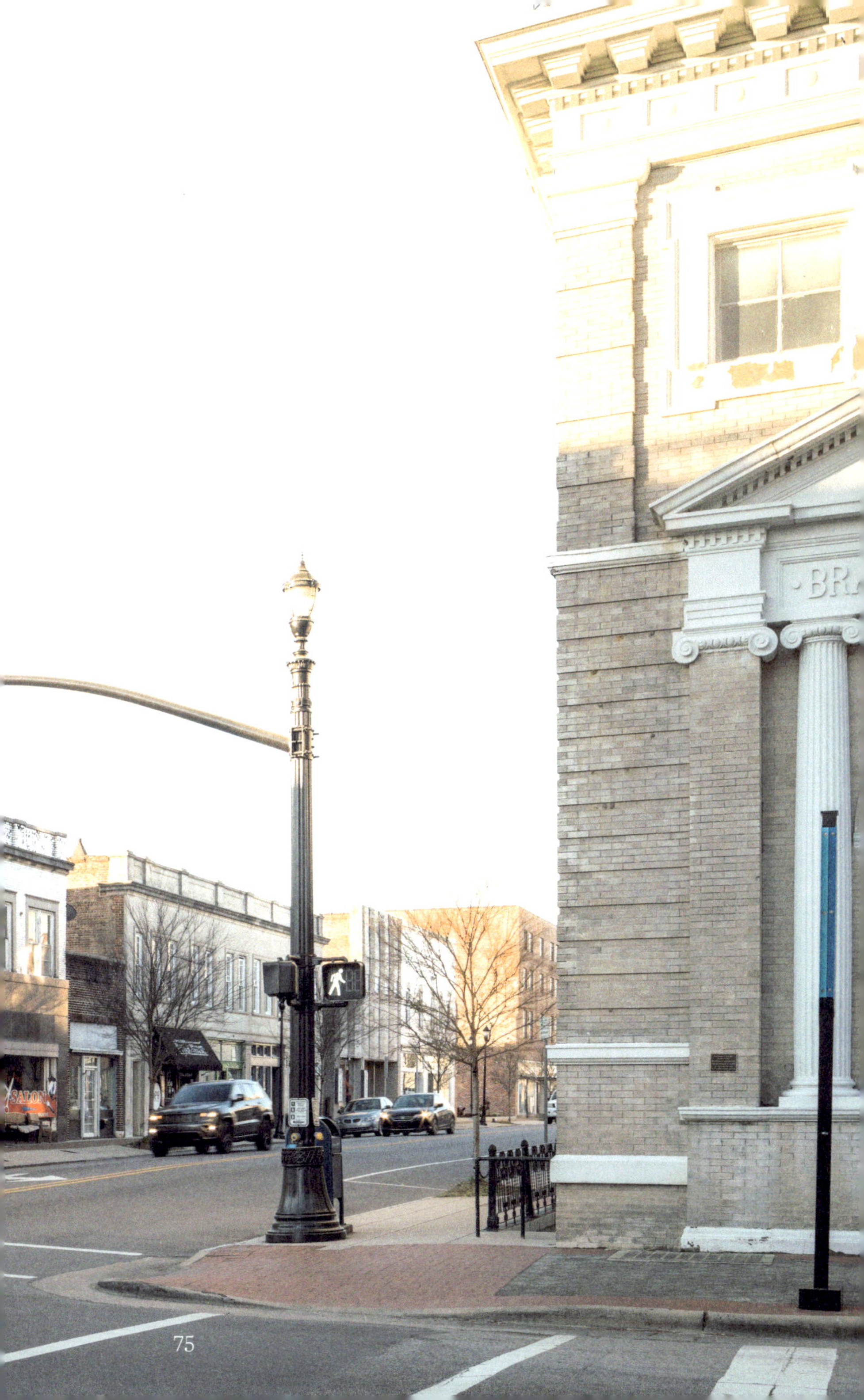
SALON
BR

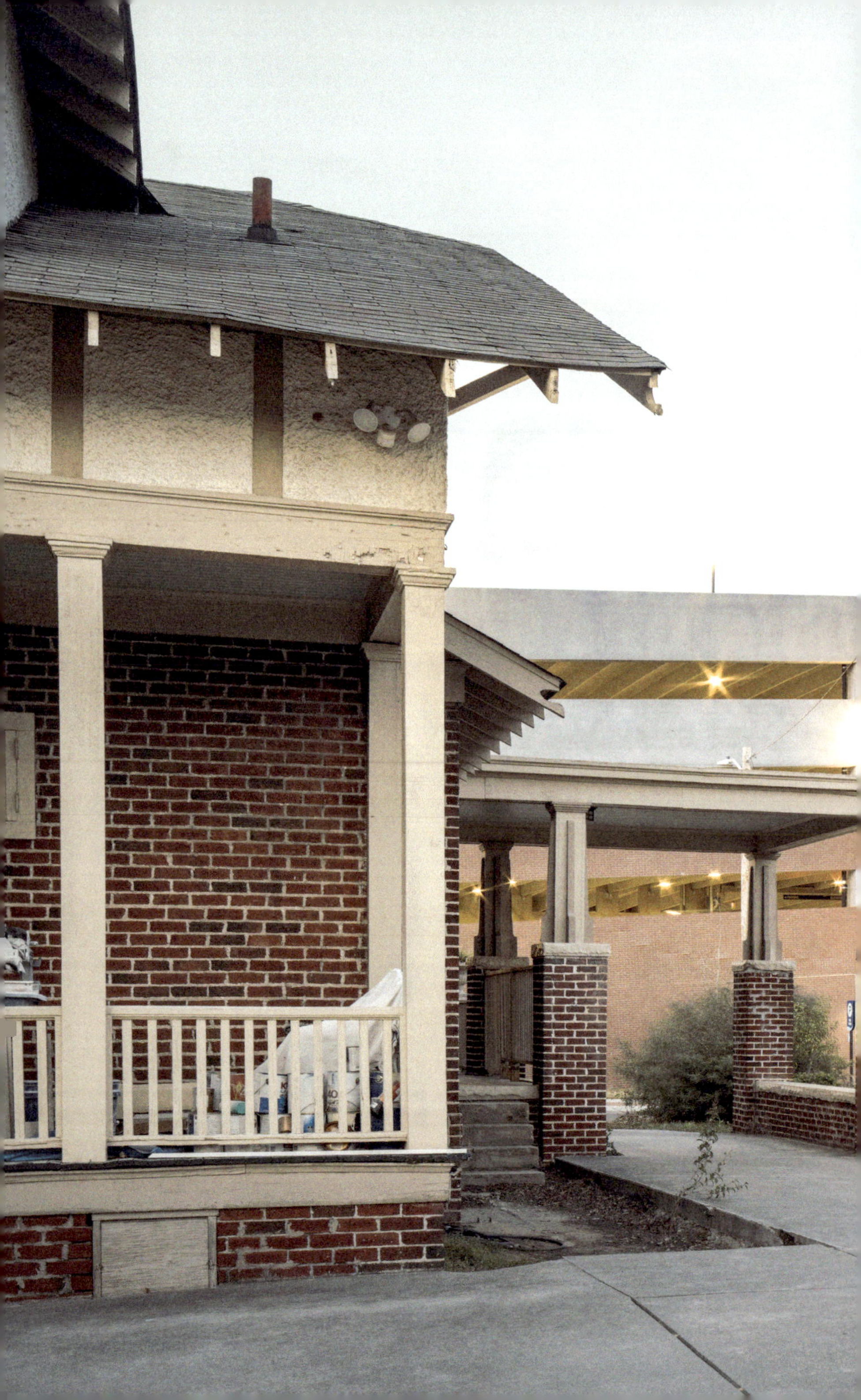

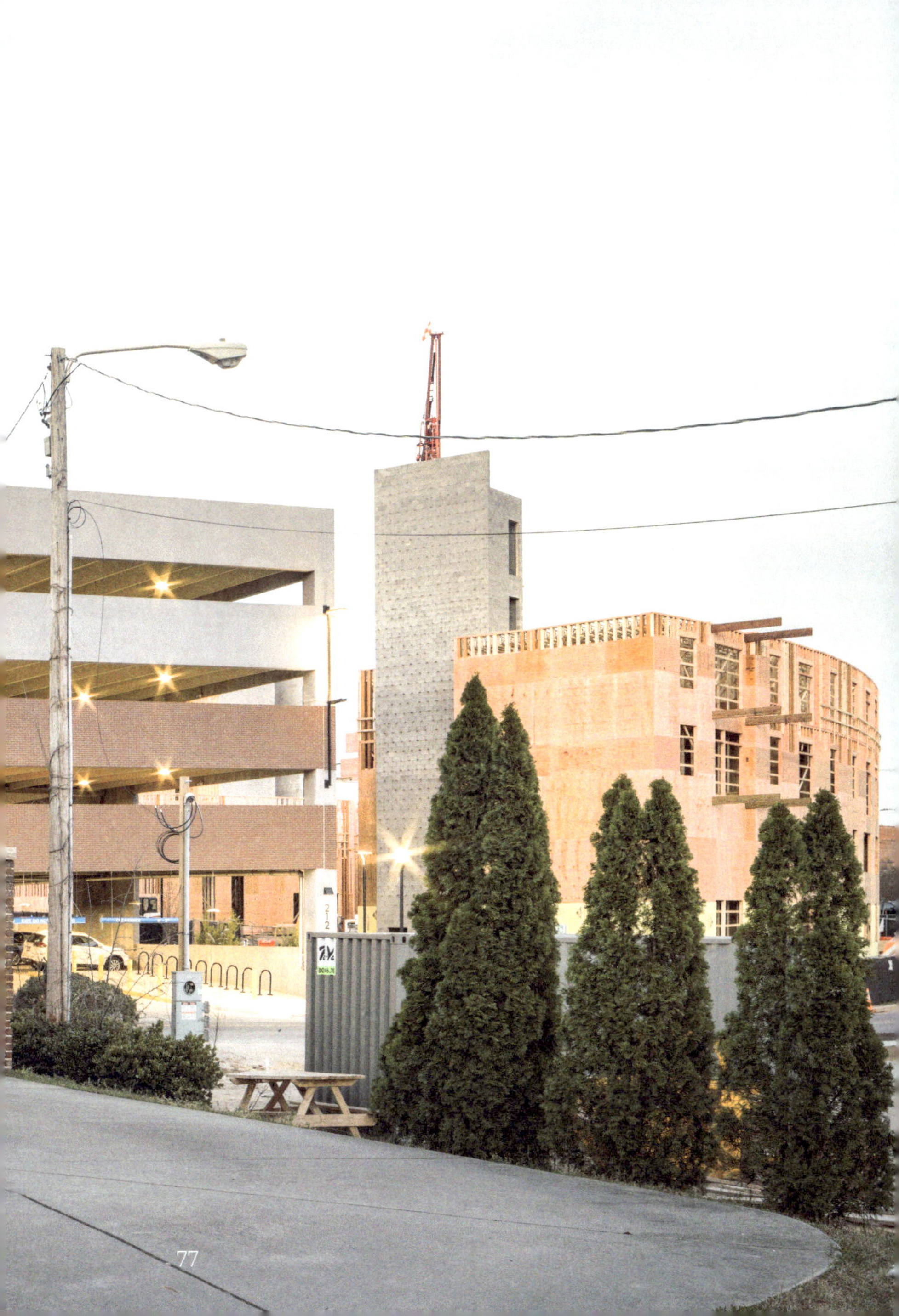

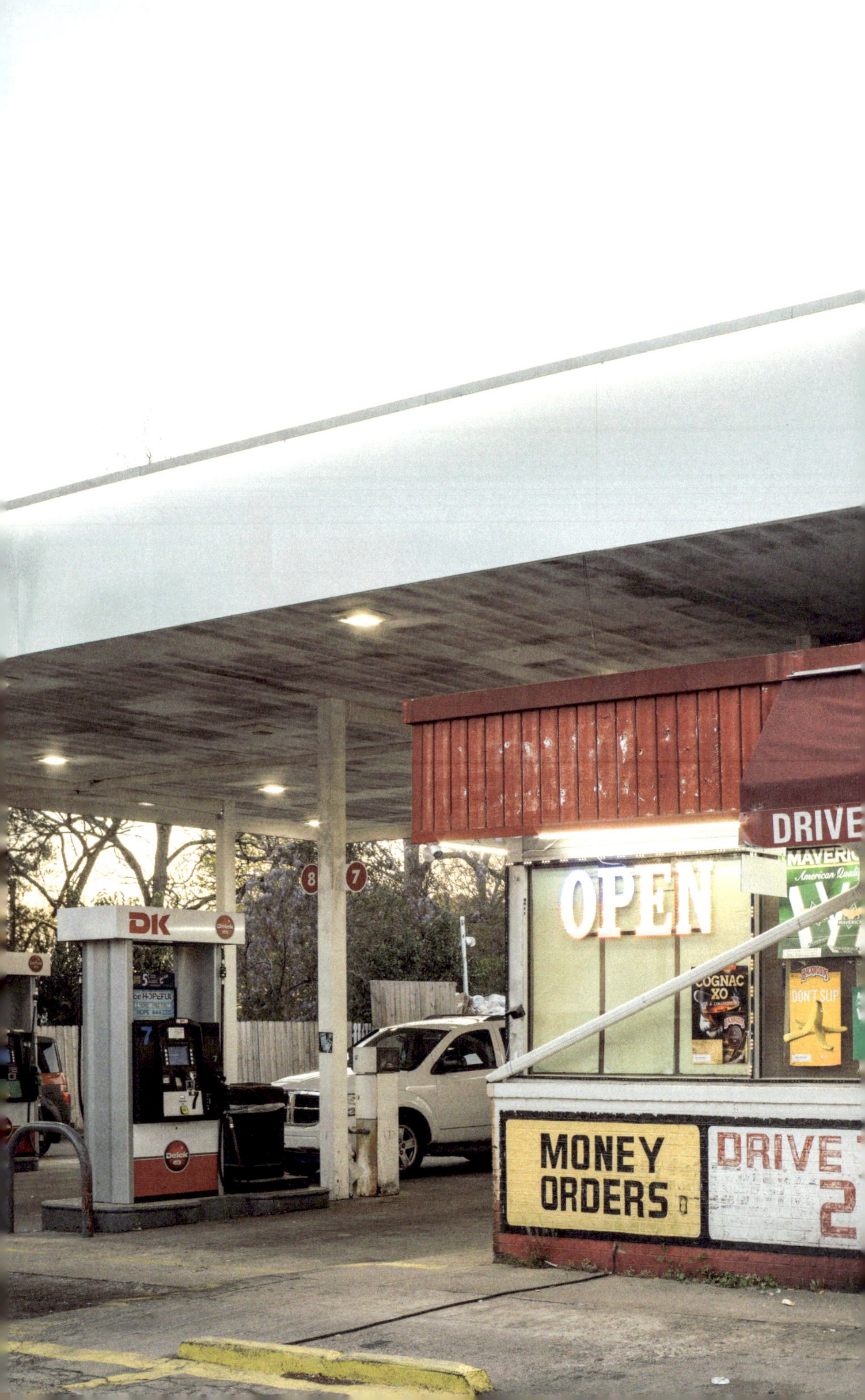
DK
OPEN
DRIVE
COGNAC XO
DON'T SLIP
MONEY ORDERS
DRIVE

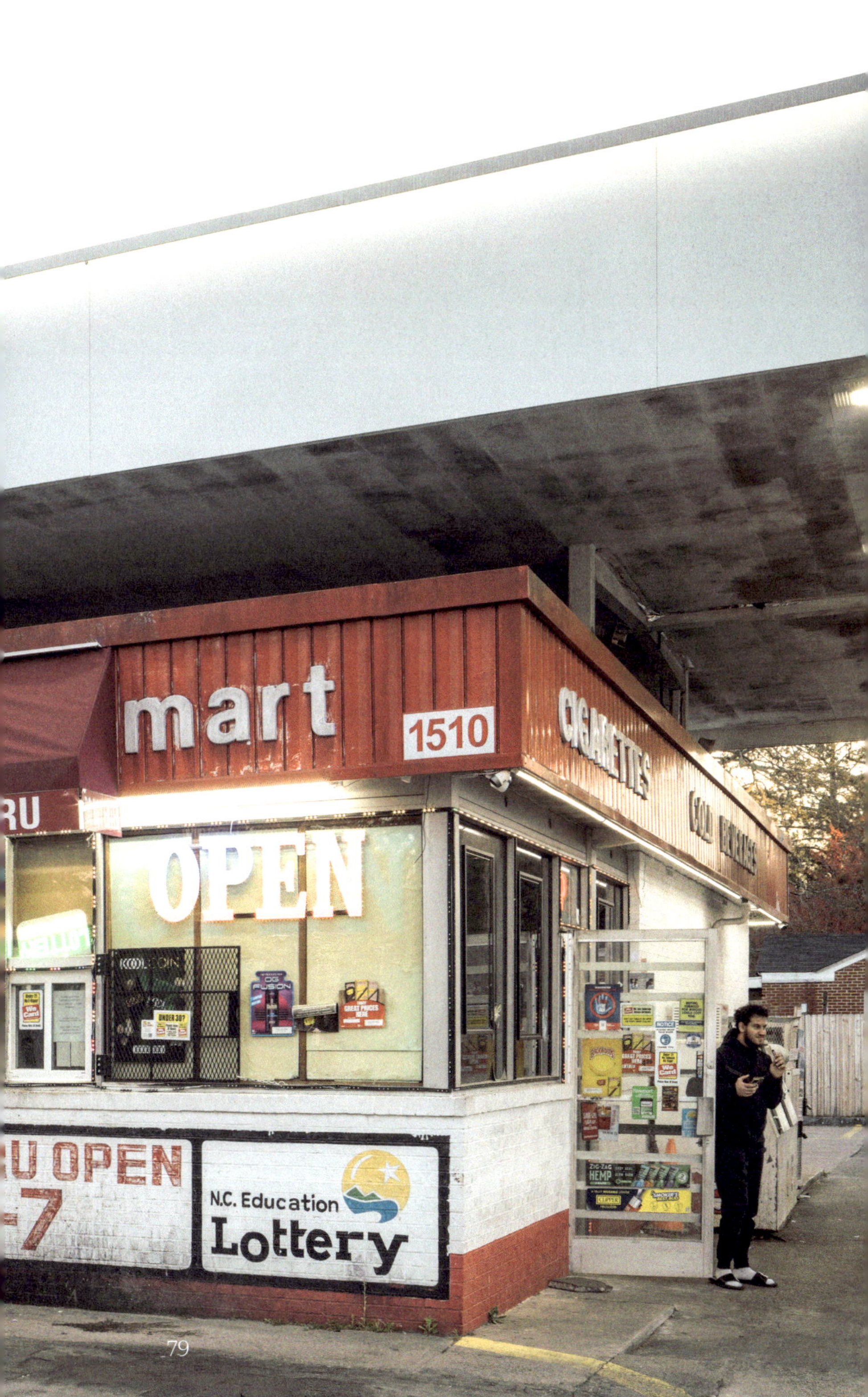
mart
1510
CIGARETTES
COLD BEVERAGES
OPEN
U OPEN
7
N.C. Education
Lottery

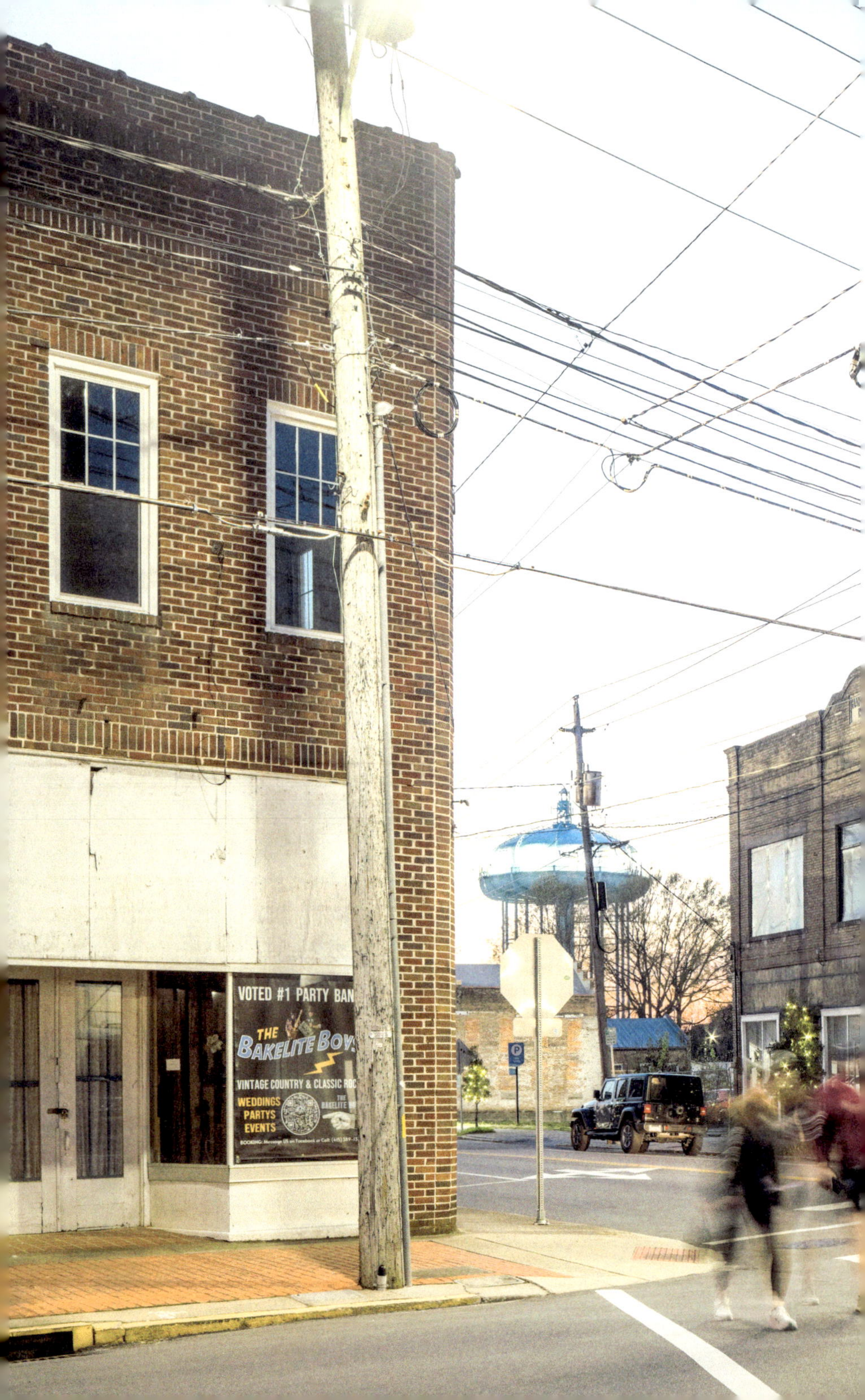
VOTED #1 PARTY BAN
THE
BAKELITE BOYS
VINTAGE COUNTRY & CLASSIC ROC
WEDDINGS
PARTYS
EVENTS
THE
BAKELITE

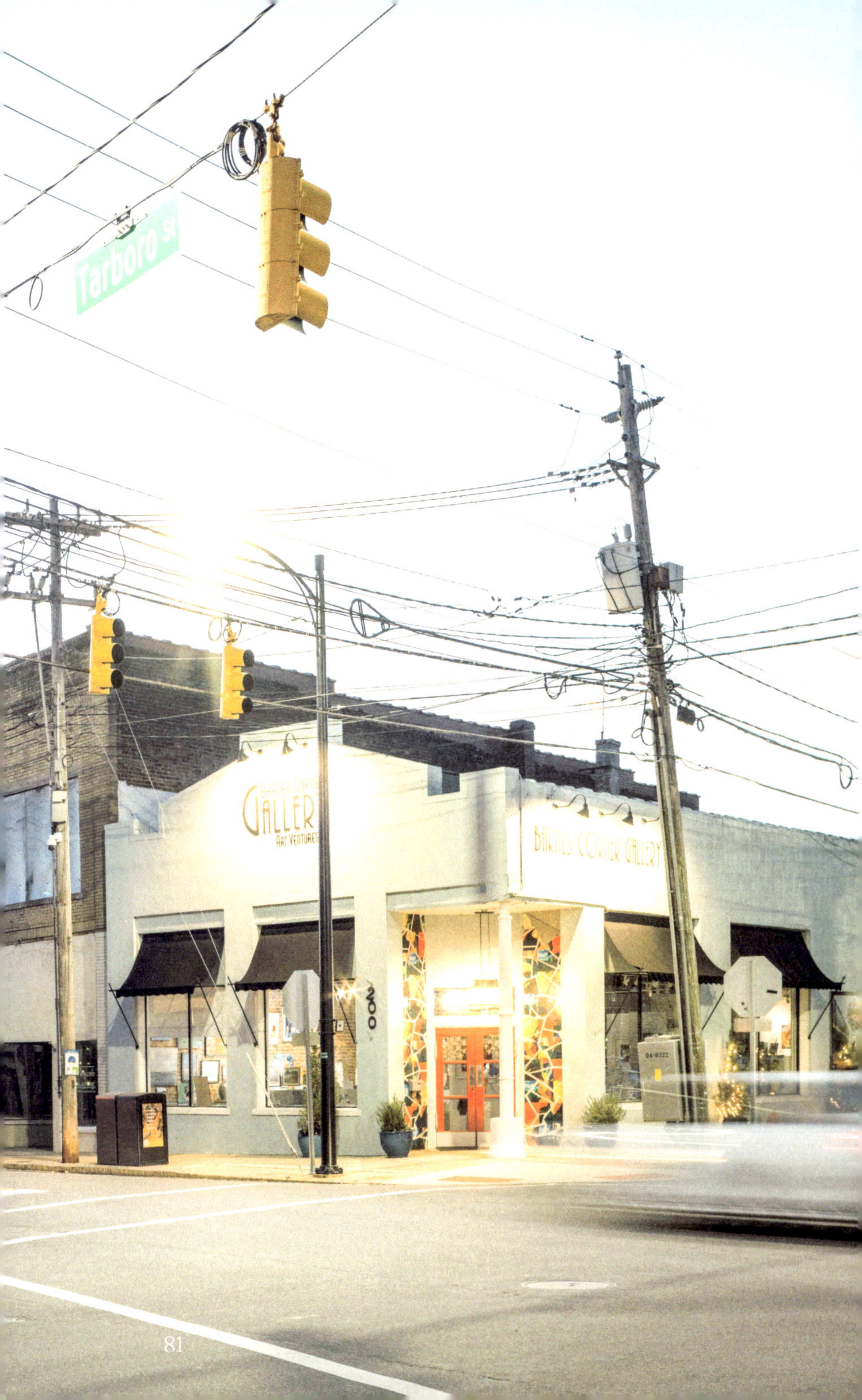
Tarboro St
BARNES CORNER GALLERY
GALLERY
ART VENTURES

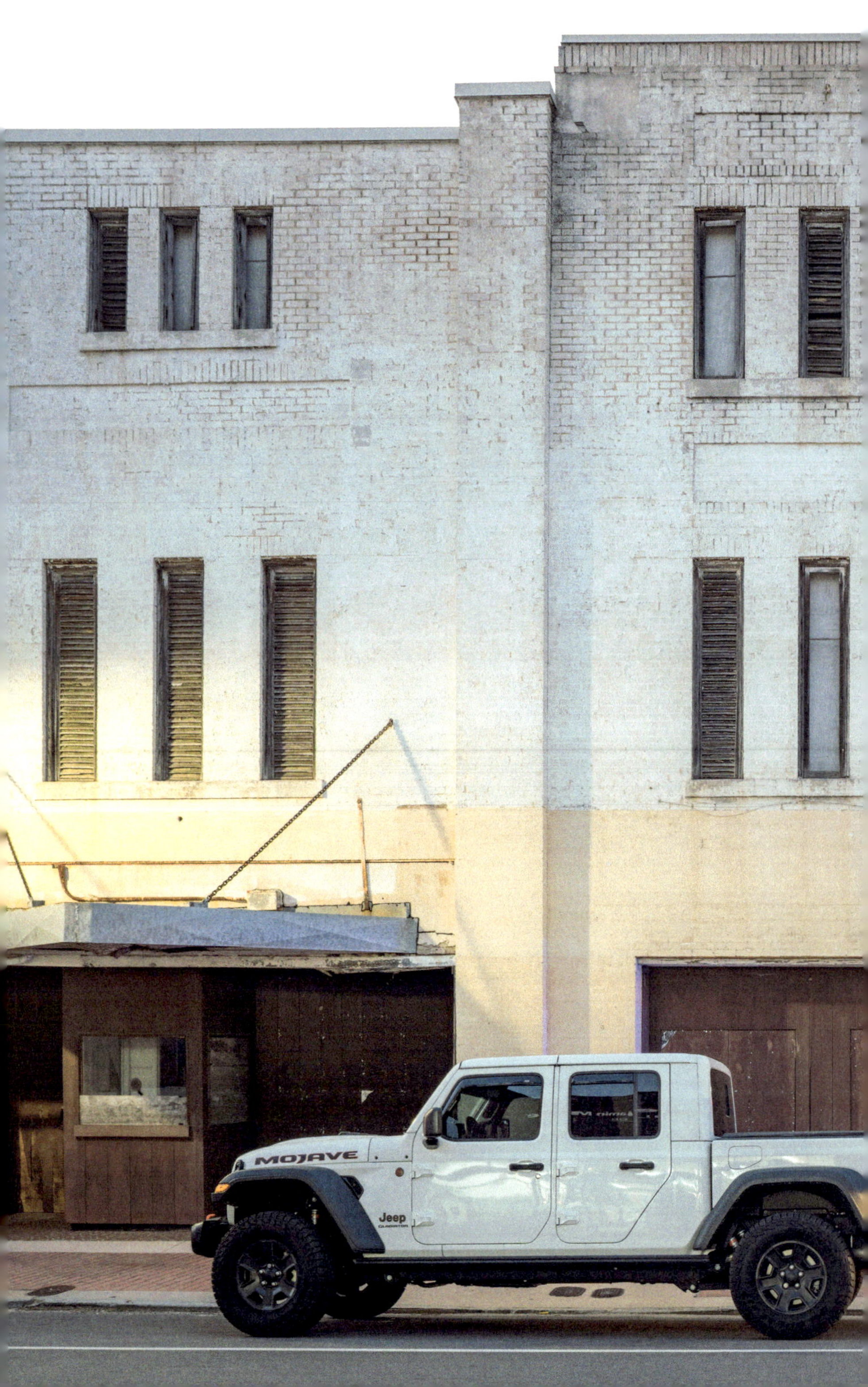
MOJAVE
Jeep

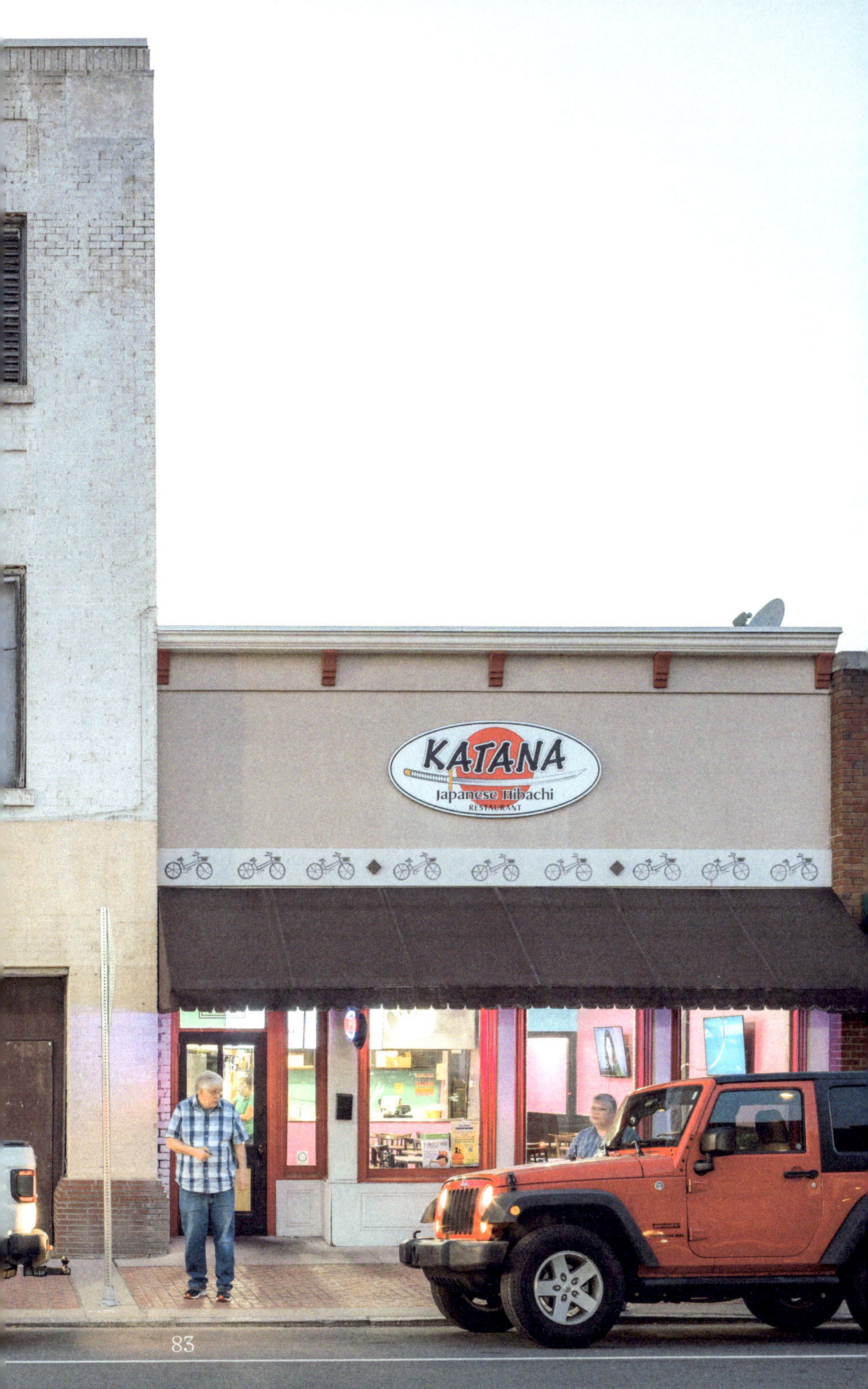
KATANA
Japanese Hibachi
RESTAURANT

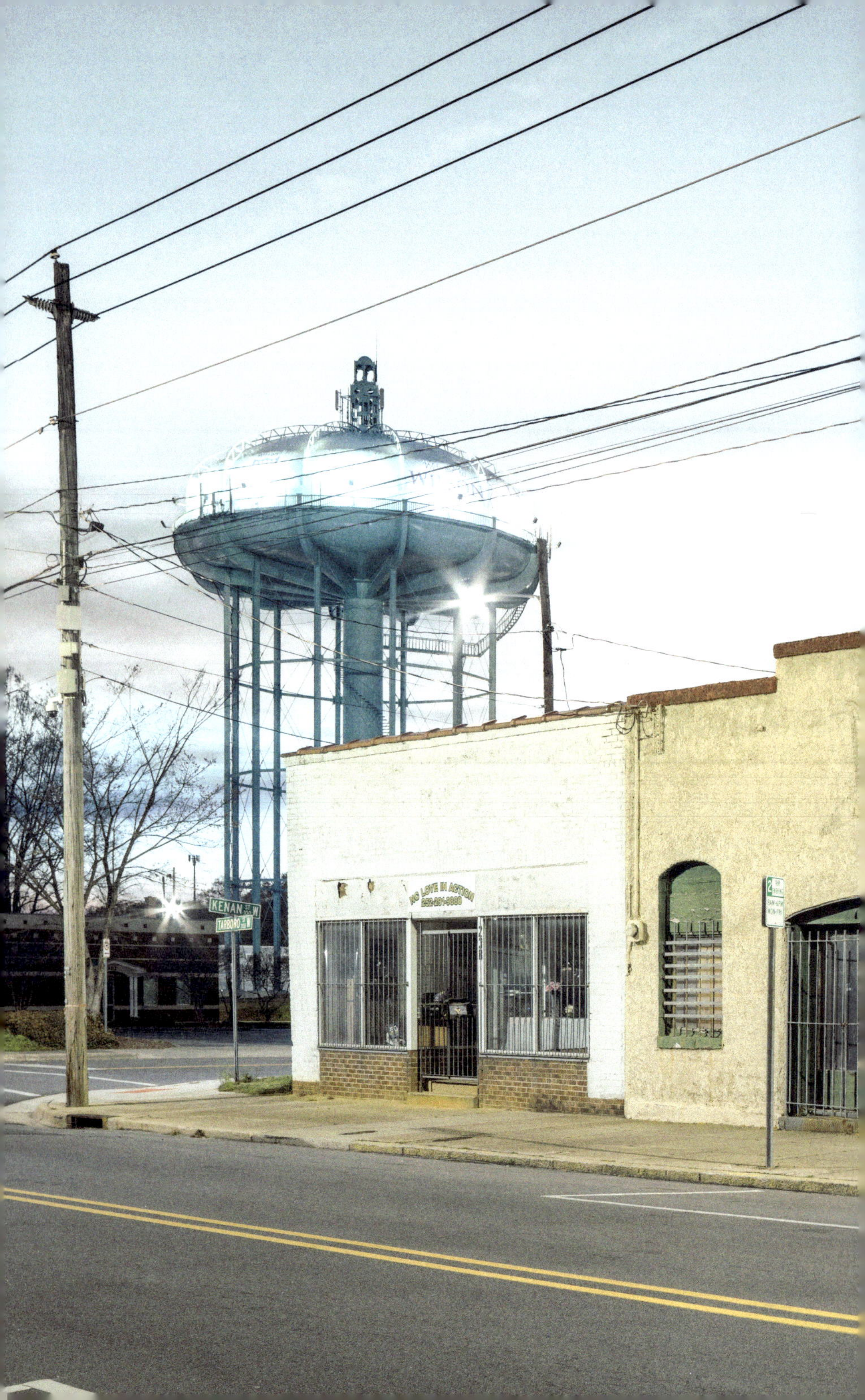
KENAN
TARBORO
NO LOVE IN ACTION

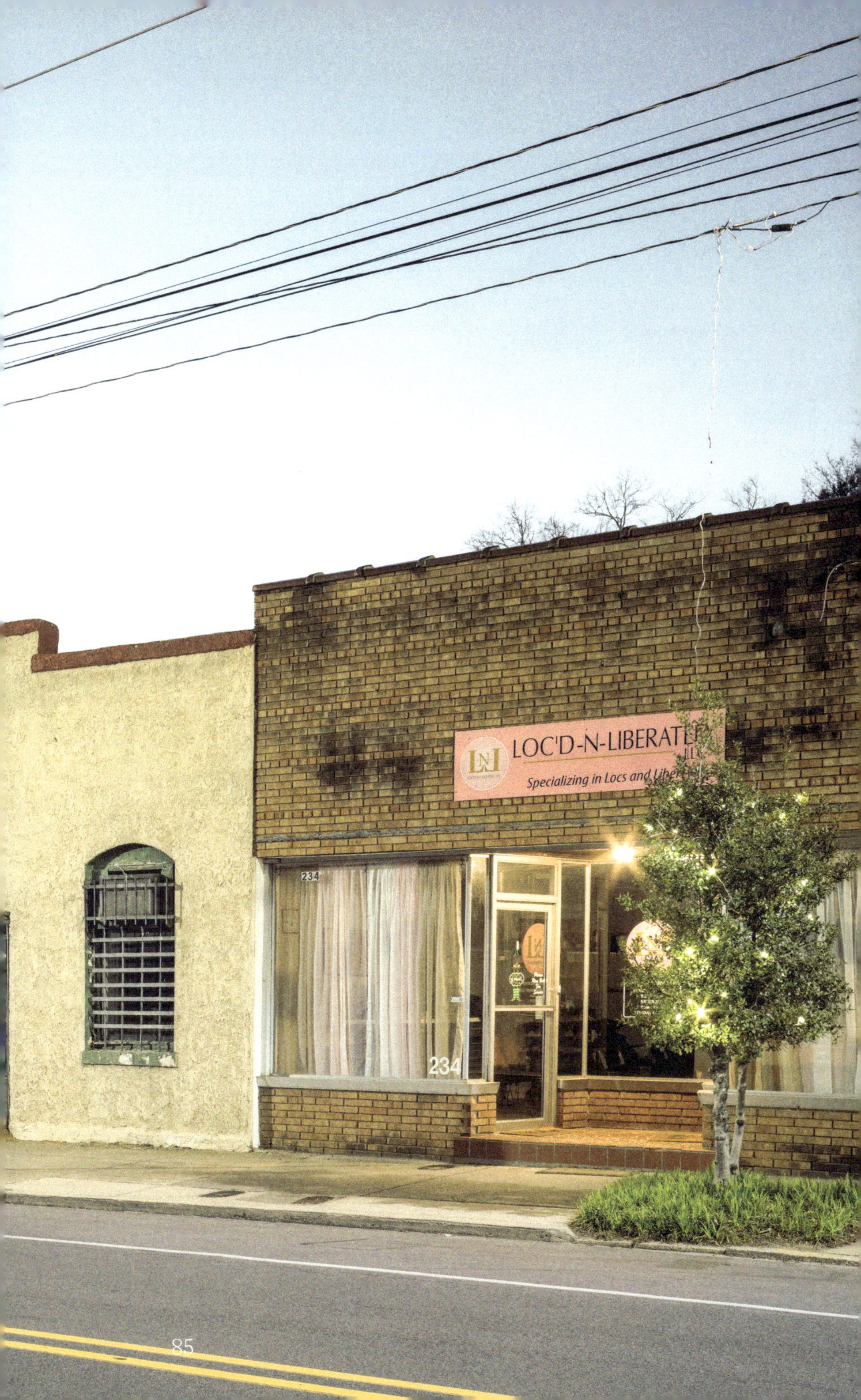
Specializing in Locs and
234
234

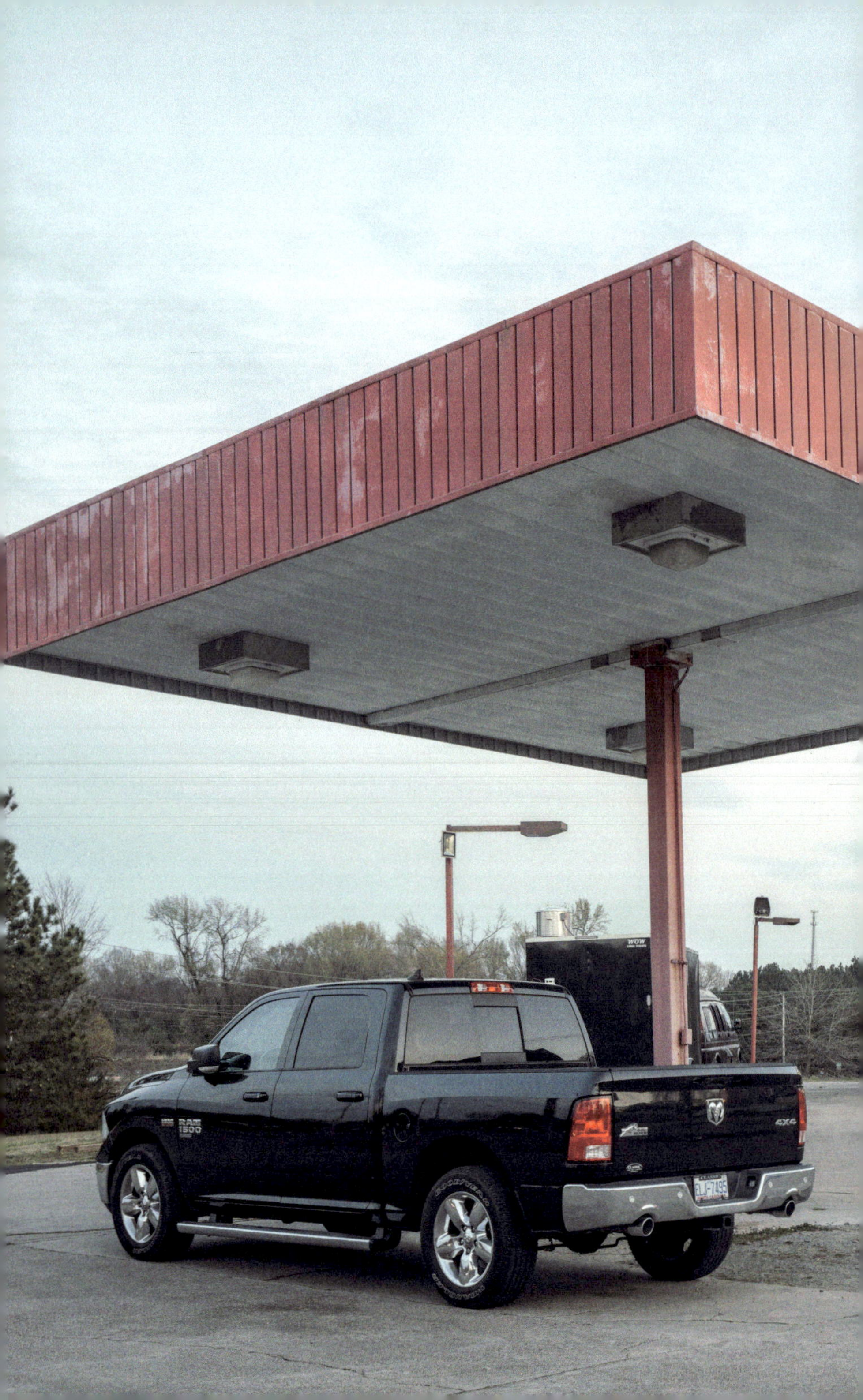
RAM
1500
4X4
WOW

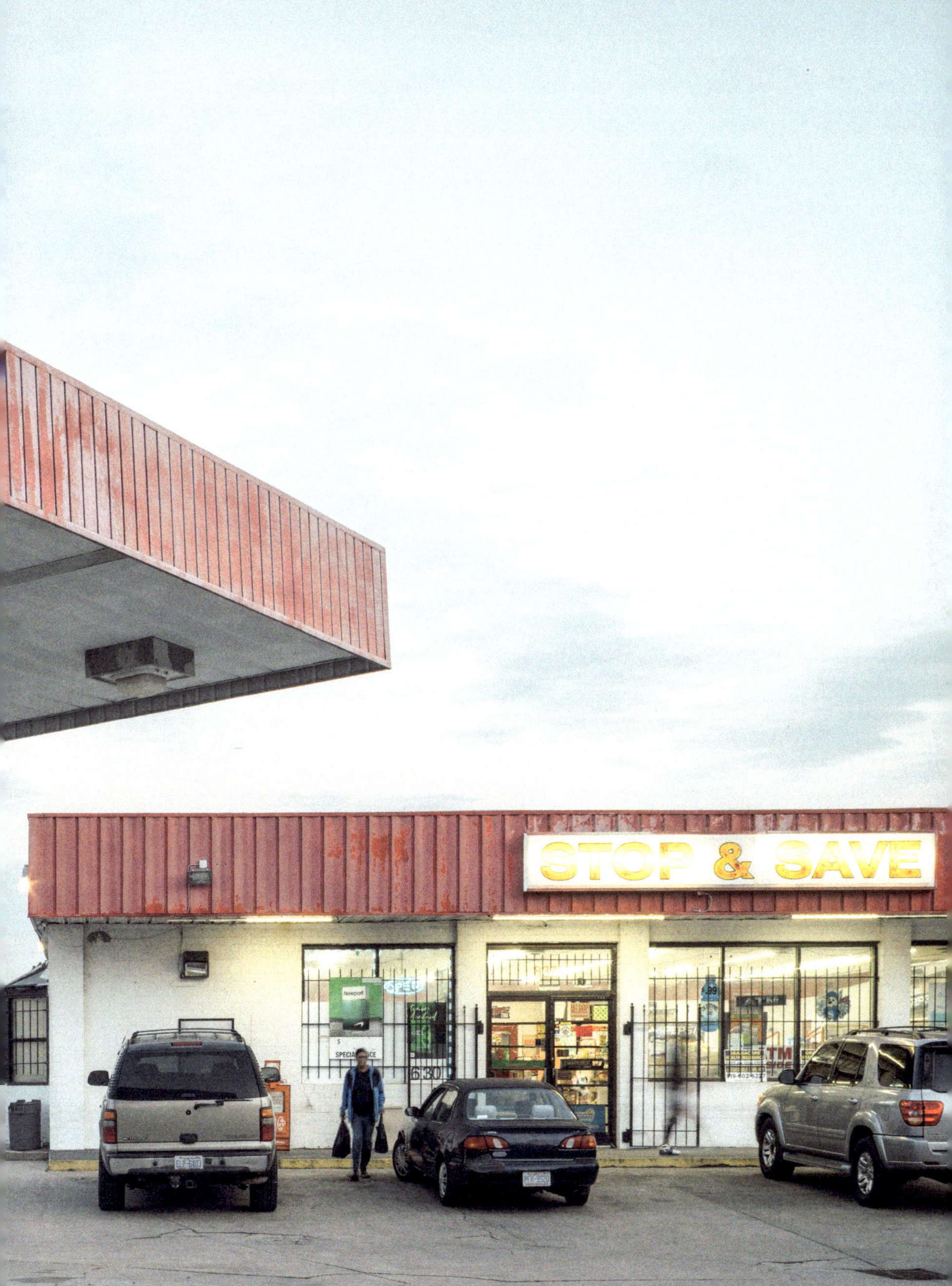
STOP & SAVE
Newport
630

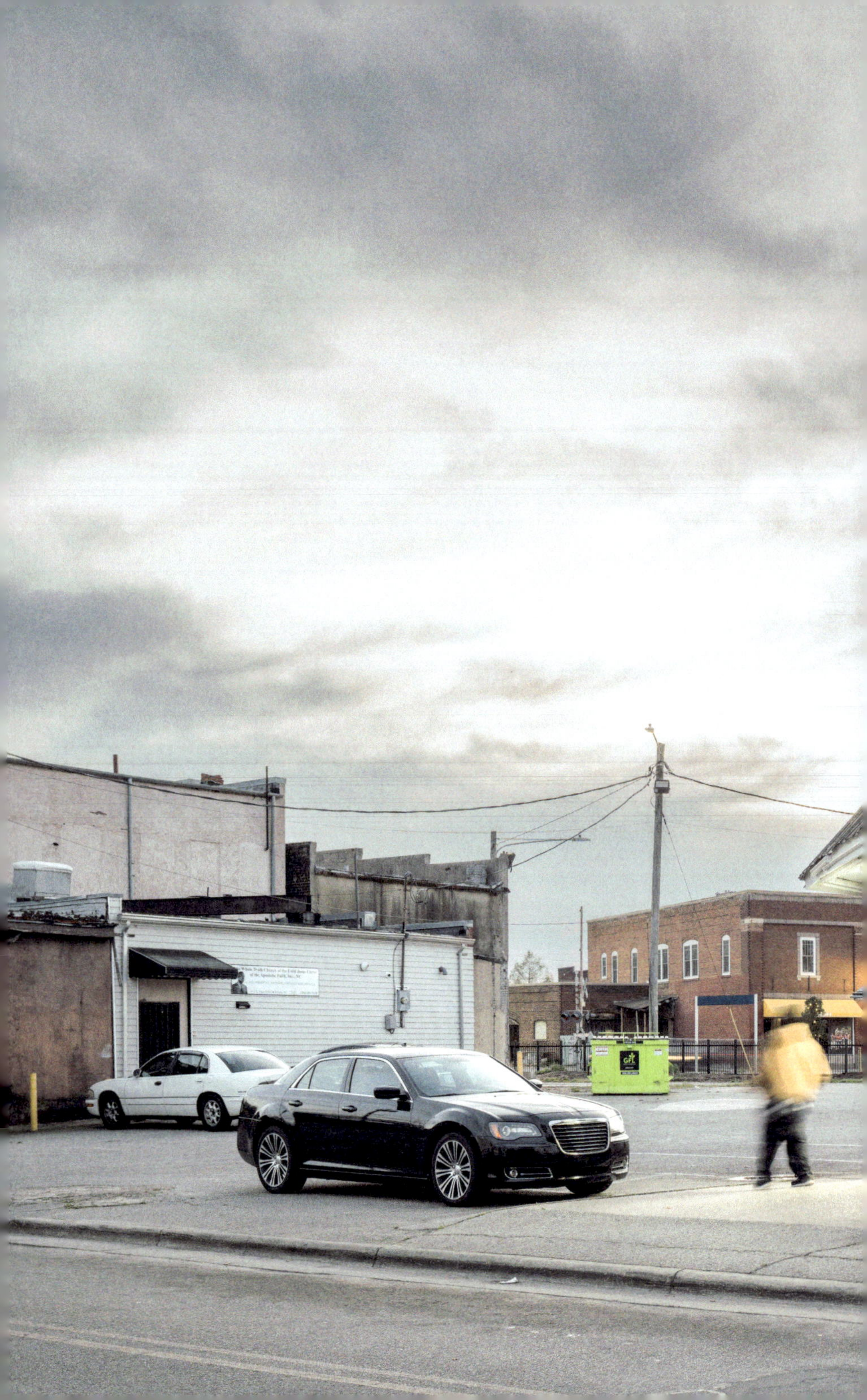

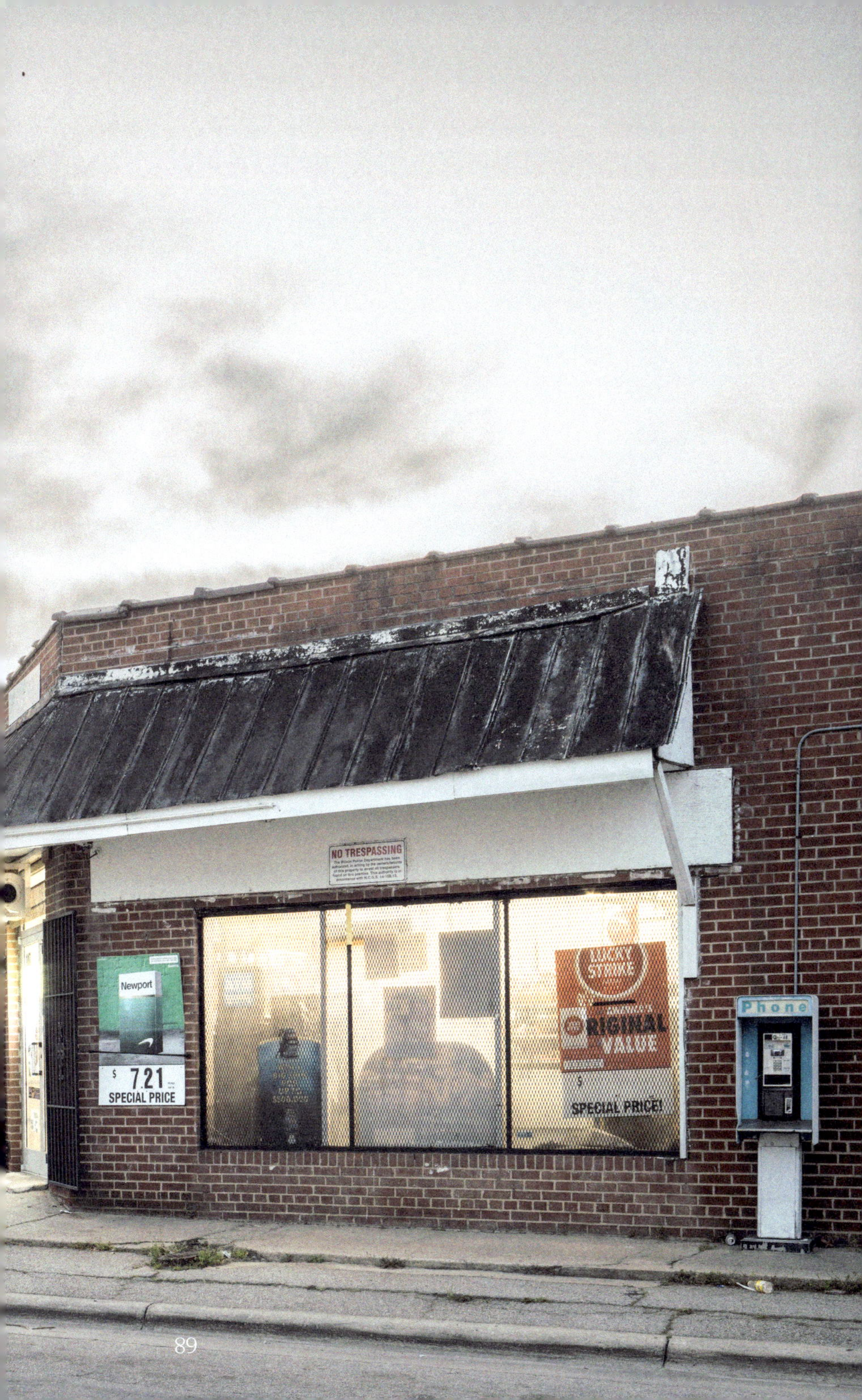
NO TRESPASSING
Newport
$ 7.21
SPECIAL PRICE
ORIGINAL
VALUE
SPECIAL PRICE!
Phone

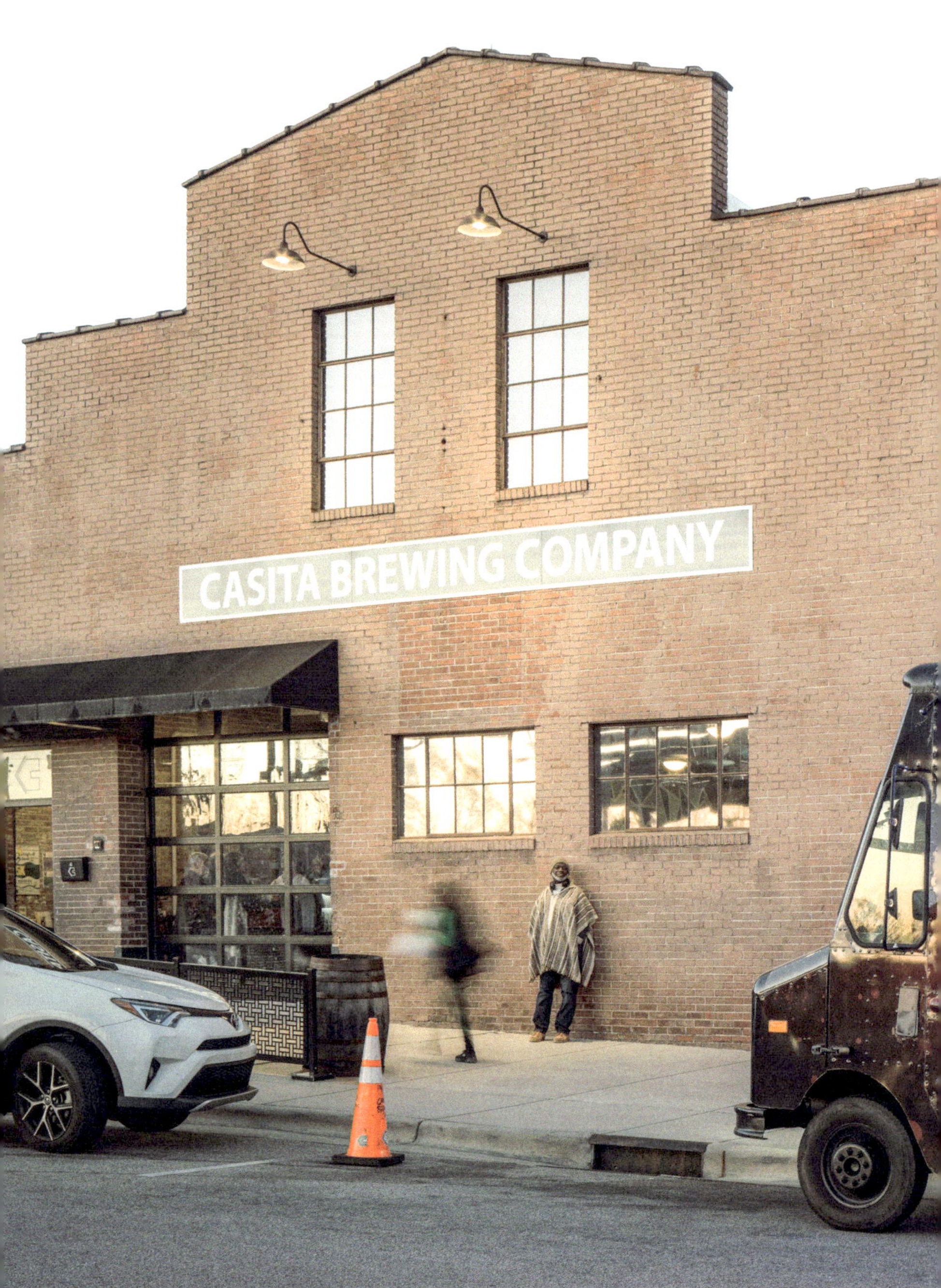
CASITA BREWING COMPANY

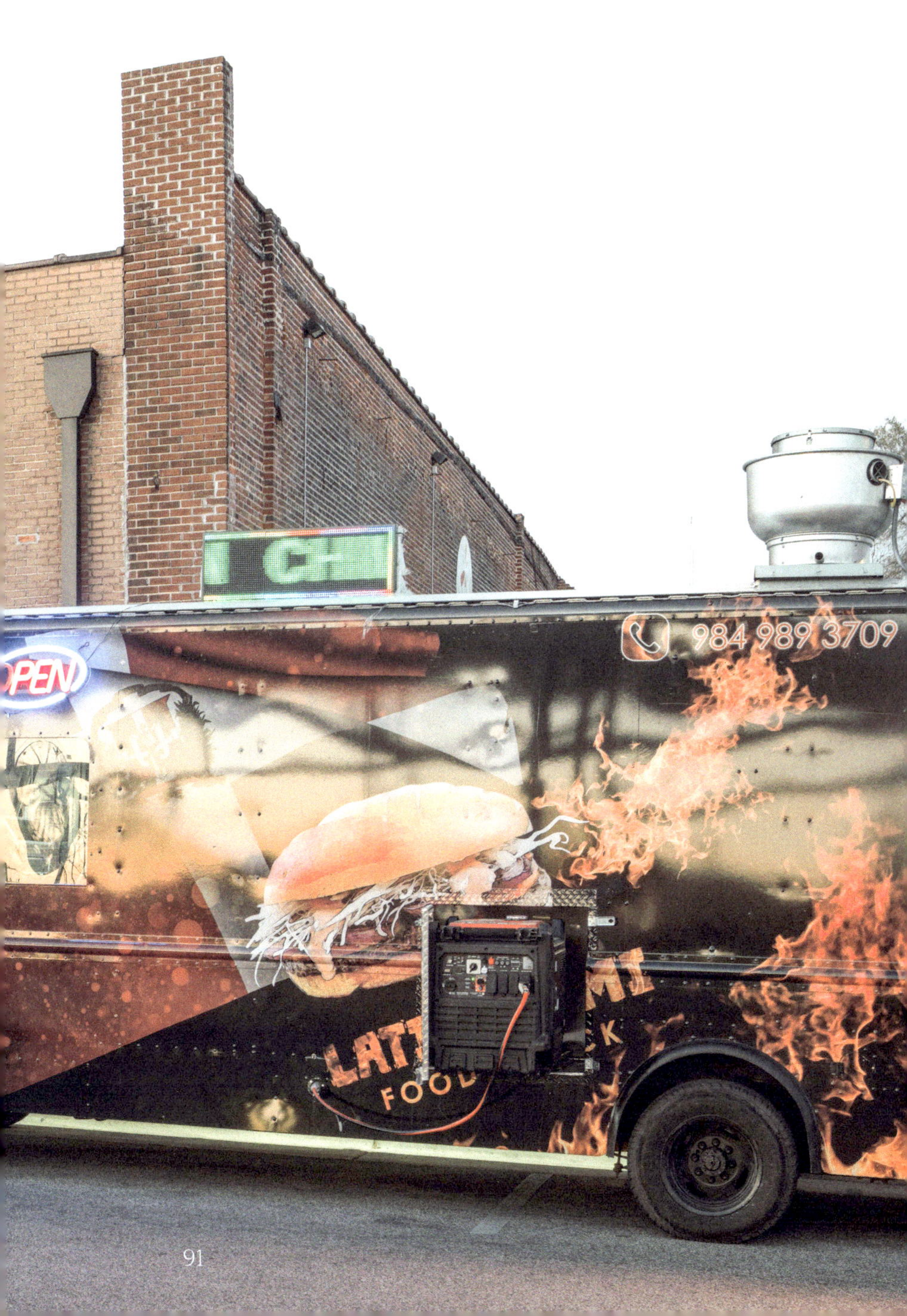
OPEN
984 989 3709

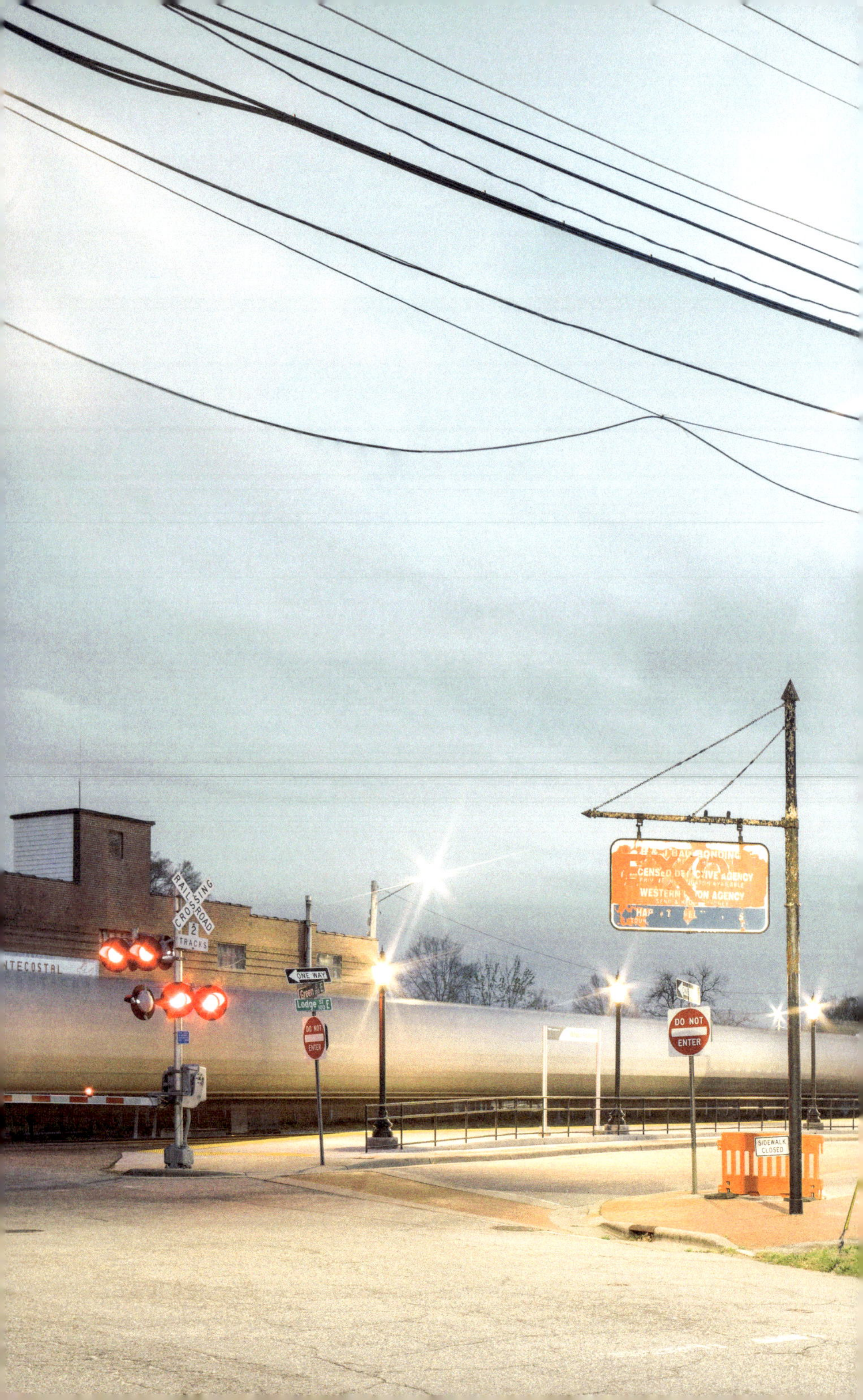
RAILROAD CROSSING
2 TRACKS
ONE WAY
Lodge
DO NOT ENTER
DO NOT ENTER
SIDEWALK CLOSED

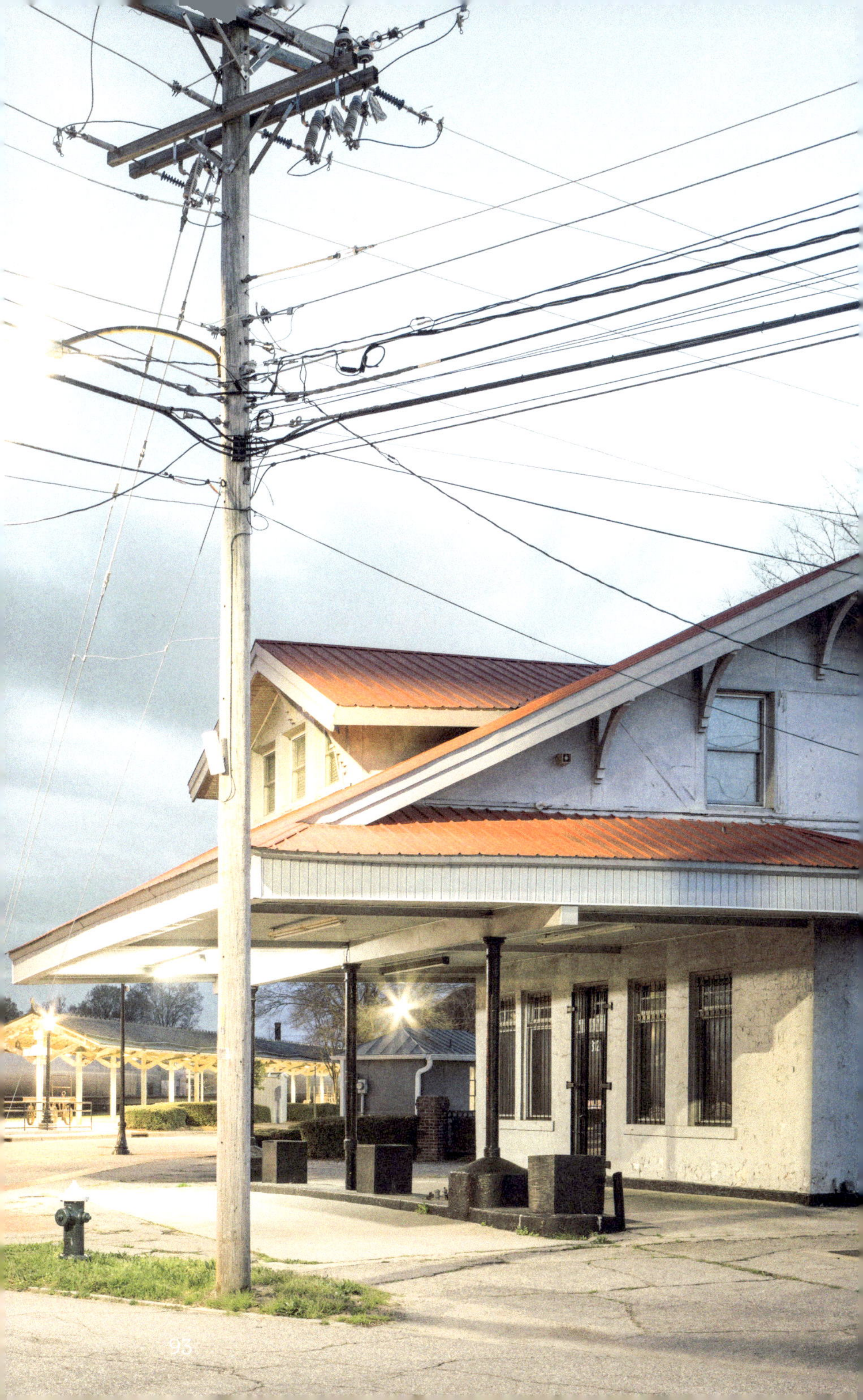

Previous Diaries

Cairo Diary #1
2014
ISBN 978-1-908889-20-1

Athens Diary #2
2015
ISBN 978-1-908889-29-4

Wolfsburg Diary #3
2016
ISBN 978-1-908889-34-8

Taipei Diary #4
2015
ISBN 978-1-908889-30-0

Kochi Diary #5
2018
ISBN 978-1-908889-44-7

Beirut Diary #6
2018
ISBN 978-1-908889-40-9

Wuhan Diary #7
2018
ISBN 978-1-908889-645

Zurich Diary #8
2019
ISBN 978-1-908889-65-2

Budapest Diary #9
2020
ISBN 978-1-908889-66-9

Osaka Diary #10
2020
ISBN 978-1-908889-56-0

Dhaka Diary #11
2021
ISBN 978-1-908889-86-7

Yangon Diary #12
2021
ISBN 978-1-908889-87-4

Minsk Diary #13
2021
ISBN 978-1-908889-88-1

Belfast Diary #14
2021
ISBN 978-1-908889-89-8

Linz Diary #15
2021
ISBN 978-1-908889-90-4

The previous diaries have been published by *thevelvetcell.com* and are available through the website.

George Town Diary #16
2022
ISBN 978-3-96070-090-6

Unna Diary #17
2022
ISBN 978-3-96070-089-0

Sarajevo Diary #18
2022
ISBN 978-3-96070-088-3

Bangkok Diary #19
2022
ISBN 978-3-96070-087-6

Kuching Diary #20
2024
ISBN 978-3-96070-105-7

Turin Diary #21
2024
ISBN 978-3-96070-103-3

Wilson Diary #22
2024
ISBN 978-3-96070-106-4

London Diary #23
2024
ISBN 978-3-96070-104-0

Wilson Diary
Peter Bialobrzeski

Published by
Hartmann Books
Liststraße 28/1
70180 Stuttgart
hartmann-books.com

Photographs
Peter Bialobrzeski
bialobrzeski.net

Graphic Design and Typesetting
Sarah Fricke, Distaff Studio

Copyediting
Tas Skorupa, New York

Printing and Binding
DZA Druckerei zu Altenburg

Paper
Pergraphica Natural Rough

Typefaces
ABC Diatype, GT Alpina

First Edition, 2024
500 copies

ISBN
978-3-96070-106-6

For Larry

This project was realized during the *Eyes on Main Street Residency*, Wilson, NC